Karl-Heinz Hermsch

Midpoint of the psyche

(How neural networks work)

© Karl-Heinz Hermsch 2023

(Revised edition)

Version: January 2026

Preliminary remark

There are, among others,

4 types, something consider.

(E.g. the content of a Non-fiction):

1. One can't understand that.

2. You don't want to understand that because it doesn't fit your own worldview. (So, not to the aims that created this.)

3. You use your cognitive abilities to understand it.

4. One has judged beforehand and thinks one understands everything.

The midpoint - mechanism is the core of the psyche.

Freedom vs. structure through one's aims

The difficulty (and impossibility) of many people to recognize the course of the midpoint - mechanics is based on their attitude:

They believe that with their "free consciousness" they determine what they take in - but do not notice that the respective aims decide this with their mechanics.

This automatically excludes what does not seem suitable.

The belief comes from the
opinion that one is free to
decide everything.

If people hold on to their old
ideas, they will continue to
go through life more or less
blindly; and will not be able
to recognize the core of their
psyche.

Prologue

In order to create something, to do something, to act, etc., you need an aim and the structure to achieve it. This is carried out by the respective neural network in the human being that is present or is formed cognitively or intuitively and what I call the **Midpoint.** (That which lies at the heart of the task.)

Depending on the aim, it can adapt or be recreated.

In order to perform it, a mechanic is activated that temporarily reduces the value of what does not match the target. This is what I call the **Midpoint-mechanic.** (The description of the process for achieving a goal using a neural network.)

This should be immediately apparent; because if everything continued to be the same, it would be harder to adapt or develop specifically for a new aim.

(One phenomenon of the center-mechanics is that it sometimes overlooks something important; it simply doesn't see it so that it cannot be considered for the solution.

However, if something is very relevant to the goal, one solution would be: to make the unseen aspect conscious through heightened attention.)

Two things are needed for implementation: Firstly, the psyche must develop the appropriate structure within oneself – and it must see the

world in a virtual state that shows a suitable path.

This is how all human behaviour works!

Why has hardly anyone seen this so far?

> ➢ Because sovereign developing and acting aims don't go with the belief in free will and the point of view that one has with his Self - control over one's psyche. (So that's how it's locked out via the mid-point mechanic).

> ➢ And that one believes to live in parallel in a metaphysical world, which leads to a blind feeling.

This is fuelled by science-detached people.

Anyone who understands the midpoint - mechanics recognizes the knitting patterns of their psyche.

And anyone who cannot (or does not want to) understand that people are guided by goals - and only goals - cannot properly perceive the midpoint - mechanics either!

And will never be able to fully understand himself.

Midpoint-mechanics

(A key to the psyche)

The midpoint is the structure that makes you an aim.

> **The function of the midpoint mechanics is generated in the psyche due to an aim to be achieved.**
>
> **This means that anything else that doesn't fit or interfere with that aim will be devalued automatically during this process.**

Midpoints are neural networks generated by aims, which then represent and execute them.

They are not rigid, but are constantly changing in terms of adapting to the environment and the inner world.

As already mentioned, other midpoints (neuron networks) that do not match are automatically reduced in value by the brain during this process.

As a rule, this is not perceived by human.

He only recognizes what the midpoints (aims) in the brain show him.

Midpoints consist of neurons distributed far and wide across the brain, which involve many areas and form a network that serves to form attitudes, actions, ideas

and especially feelings

to create.

Feelings form in order to be able to react quickly in similar situations.

In addition, they develop fine adjustments for situations and tasks.

Since the beginning of all life, it has been controlled by emo- tions.

Hence their strong role, even in today's world.

Depending on the flexibility of the respective brain, there are always new
networks in addition to the existing
ones, which are formed, i.e. by adapting to the outside or inside world
(lightning-fast or gradually).

Other midpoints are changed or closed
for these reasons.

While everything in the universe is
shaped by aims who "don't care" about
the consequences of structure, with

living beings the aim of preservation is added (to survive).

This takes place in the brain through networks of neurons, glial cells and synapses, which I call "midpoints". Depending on the type and individual, the living beings are shaped by them.

As a general knitting pattern, the example of how to learn to ride a bike:

In the beginning there is the aim. This creates a neural network in the brain to reach it.

Balance, muscles, tendons, posture, mental processes, etc. are developed as sub-aims in the required form, coordinated with one another and temporarily stored.

So gradually the skills are improved; you learn from your mistakes.

This is all done by the neural networks formed by the aim of cycling and then further evolving to expand body-psyche coordination and fine-tune adjustments.

The network at the beginning (the midpoint of cycling) has now become far-reaching interdependencies. Which, when the respective sub-aims have been achieved, are stored permanently and become an automatic behaviour that is activated when you get back on the bike.

Midpoints are thus created by aims and are their tools.

Neural networks connect areas of the brain such as: frontal lobe, cerebral cortex, cerebellum, limbic system, amygdala, language midpoint, visual cortex, hearing center, taste center, etc., and access memory content and everything that goes with it.

There is also a constant exchange of information with the autonomic nervous system (plus the somatic nervous system) and the enteric nervous system (which is also called the 'abdominal brain').

Midpoints act in such a way that they allow everything that could help to achieve or maintain their structure - the aim - and do not take everything else into account as far as possible.

This usually continues unconsciously.

Anyone who becomes aware of this mechanism also understands a lot about how their own psyche works.

In general, the midpoints play the concert of life with one another; many processes take place at the same time.

In extreme cases, however, one midpoint can greatly reduce all the others so that only this midpoint shapes people, for example in phases of panic, ecstasy or when one is about to achieve maximum performance.

But even in the spectrum between normal and extreme, all midpoints act in such a way that they limit or strengthen others in value.

Another reason why it is so difficult to explain the midpoint mechanics to other people is that they are always on some aim without really realizing it. They cannot or do not see their psychological processes.

What is even less perceived is that a lot no longer plays a role due to the respective aim.

One should perhaps have had the experience that one's view of the world can change in fractions of a second in order to understand it better.

I formed the term "midpoint-mechanics" in order not to always use neural-network-laws. It makes clearer in a more memorable way that a neural network mechanically reduces or strengthens others in value, depending, as I said, whether they are unsuitable or suitable for the current midpoint.

And one more hint:

> **Most explanations of how the brain works boil down to certain areas being activated and responding to stimuli.**

But never just one area reacts; rather a neuron network (which connects different sub-areas via synapses) is always

activated by the stimuli, which communicates with others. Because of course not the whole area is used, but only a part, which is usually not strictly limited, but is dependent on the other neuron network.

You could compare it to preparing a meal:

Knowledge plays an important role. In other words, what you need in what quantity, which procedure must be followed, what the hands or devices have to do, what amount of energy is required, whether the taste is right, etc. All of this works together in the right amount and forms that Meal.

Applied to the work of the brain to achieve a goal, this means that each brain area contributes a limited part that activates the responsible neural network in order to come to a successful conclusion.

Just as the ingredients etc. are not used without restriction, so is the brain. Here a neural network is in charge, there the recipe.

Perhaps the terms "selective attention" and "flow" will help you understand better. In the first, only certain information that fits a goal is perceived from a large number of pieces of information. With the second one is in a flow that is only determined by one goal and does not allow anything else, i.e. is not disturbed by anything.

Both also apply to the midpoint-mechanics. Here, however, there is also the reference to the strict regularity with which perception is restricted. This means that the brain only perceives what is essential for the respective aim or aims. Everything else is absolutely not noticed and is virtually non-existent.

So, nothing is rated negatively or suppressed (accordingly, it does not trigger any reactions). So, the process is not disturbed by anything; one only lives in the world of the respective aim.

Without the midpoint mechanics, the brain would plunge into chaos because aims could no longer be pursued permanently.

As I said, it is relatively seldom that people are shaped by only one midpoint. As a rule, many processes take place at the same time, all of which run according to the midpoint-mechanics and, depending on their value, are more or less important for other aims. This creates for example certain clusters that execute processes together.

In one sentence:

The more the brain pursues an aim, the less there will be other aims that do not contribute to it can, perceived or can work.

> This is presented again in great detail in the **conversation about the midpoint mechanics at the end of this book.**

In this context, the experiment with a large number of people with a video of 75 seconds duration that the scientists Simons and Chabris carried out and called it "gorillas in our midst" is perhaps also interesting:

The film shows two teams with three players each, one wearing white and the other black T-shirts. The members of each team play a normal orange basketball by throwing or dribbling. After 44 to 48 seconds, something unexpected happens: a smaller person, completely wrapped in a gorilla costume, walks across the screen in the same way as the players. During these unexpected events, the basketball players unwaveringly continue their actions.

Before the test subjects see a video, they are given the task of either concentrating on the team in white or on the team in black and counting all rallies of the observed team in their heads or counting the thrown and dribbled rallies separately. After the test subjects have seen the video and completed their observation task, they are asked to write down their numbers. Then you ask them if (a) they noticed something unusual while counting, (b) if they noticed anything other than the six players, if someone else appeared in the video, finally: (c) Do you have a gorilla see going through the picture?

About half of the subjects did not notice the gorilla.

My comment on this: The given aims (the midpoints) did not allow everything else (including the gorilla) to be perceived.

On the basis of this experiment one can clearly see how a midpoint - here the task - works.

And one more note: wizards and hypnotists all work with the midpoint-mechanics.

Finally:

Who hasn't wondered why people can do something that goes far beyond "normal" behaviour - in a positive or negative way.

Here, too, the midpoint mechanism is the key to understanding it.

Because with it you can make all extreme behaviours clear.

Just as everything has two sides, so does the midpoint - mechanism:

Neural networks can form (negative) complexes that lead to unhealthy behaviour and block out criticism of it because it would endanger "comfort zones."

Complexes are tightly closed units that do not let anything else in; they react extremely stubbornly to attempts at change.

Two small examples for better understanding:

▸ You are talking to someone about a topic (so you are in the midpoint of it). Suddenly you have the feeling that the other person is insulting you.

This can result in a new midpoint emerging, which weakens the previous one.

▸ You are on your way to work and thinking about the tasks ahead of you.

Suddenly you witness a robbery and are now in this midpoint (with your mind).

If you later look back at your altered state, you will find that the raid suddenly eliminated all previous thoughts. This new midpoint has reduced everything else to zero.

Appendix

Non-perception due to the midpoint - mechanism

vs. repression

"If you say: 'A midpoint prevents you from perceiving something', then you get to the point much more accurately than if you say: 'You have repressed something'."

"I understood it like this," CP summed up: "An aim has to be achieved. To do this, a certain structure is needed. This is created from what is relevant to it, everything else is ignored. If something is disturbing, its value is reduced, so it has much less influence on the person."

I nodded. "This reduction of the other values does not happen intentionally, but mechanically.

It is a lawful process. That is why I called it 'midpoint - mechanism'.

An example: On March 24, 2015, a pilot committed suicide in a passenger plane. He steered the plane into a rock massif. He took all 150 passengers with him to their deaths.

What was going on in this person's head?

The answer is provided by the midpoint - mechanism: the aim of taking one's own life reduced the value of all other midpoints (aims) or reduced them to zero; the impending collision with the mountains, the people who were on board and had to die with him, their relatives who had to suffer the loss, etc.

On the one hand, it is frightening what midpoints can do, including the terrible atrocities of the Nazi regime or inhumane acts that virtually all peoples committed."

"Or what individual people did to others," added CP.

"Yes. On the other hand, it is beautiful what midpoints can do. For example, love, standing up for people or other living beings.

"What can you do to escape a negative focus, not to be a slave to it and to expand your perception?"

"In quiet moments, look closely at it and ask yourself what aim is behind it.

Then: create a counter-aim and link it to the midpoint. That means: create a new aim that is activated every time the impulse tries to provoke negative behaviour, and thus dampens and regulates it, influencing your own behaviour more and more.

Psyche

Since people are shaped by aims, it is clear what it consists of.

▶How did it come about?

When life developed from matter, it wanted to continue to exist.

▶ What is its task?

It strives to carry out the aims inherent in each living being. The psyche serves to preserve life by adapting to the environment, including through feeling, thinking, learning.

▶ How does it work?

Through aims that have created neural network connections.

▶ Where is the psyche?

In the brain.

(Wikipedia definition: The brain is an organ of the central nervous system of all vertebrates and some invertebrates, which consists primarily of nerve tissue.)

The central point of all life is the command anchored in the psyche to follow one's feelings - especially the life instinct. It was formed around 3.5 billion years ago and continues to have an effect today.

> **The psyche therefore consists of the aims that are in the human brain, or that are formed and that move the person with the resulting centers, unconsciously or consciously.**

With regard to activity, which depends on the state and course of the external world and the state of the internal states, there are centers that act in the foreground or background and those that are currently passive (e.g. centers are ostensibly active in a new environment, social behaviors take place in the background in parallel, and passive are aims that are satisfied or not needed at the moment).

The midpoints are initially generated by aims and represent them. This means that if a neural network is stimulated, the goal is activated.

Depending on the demands of life, new aims are constantly formed that generate midpoints.

(The processes of learning and unlearning take place in the synapses of the neurons).

Midpoints can become stronger or weaker in value - depending on when and how often they are needed. If they are no longer needed, they weaken and usually die out.

Psychological phenomena or functions, i.e. acts, states, patterns, experiences, are generally the effects of neural networks that work together with other midpoints and generate feelings in parallel.

The midpoints are networked with each other depending on the aims, can form clusters (a grouping for certain processes) and usually always learn something new.

This means that the psyche in the brain remains flexible and adaptable.

The psyche is not the same as the soul, because it believes in super naturalistic elements.

Of course, faith can also be a center in the psyche and thus influence other neural networks.

This particularly applies to religious, mystical themes, which can cause a self-fulfilling prophecy in the person concerned through the resulting perspective, which can change their psyche and subsequently their body.

Psychological satisfaction and balance are evident when the midpoints harmonize with each other.

More or less imbalance arises, for example, when aims with their centers negatively influence the function of others beyond a healthy level. Or cannot be achieved. This can occur due to expectations that are too high.

Here you could say: satisfaction is usually based on the level of expectations.

So, if you are dissatisfied, you should look for the aims - and possibly modify them (change them or replace them with another aim).

Sleep and dreams create different patterns in the psyche because brain functions then work differently.

What the MIND is

> **The mind is based on the human psyche: the mid-points and in these the search for facts.**

Driven by new or existing aims, the mind can jump from one neural network to other at lightning speed in order to track down information on how to achieve them.
These are temporarily stored in the new network that may have been created by the respective aim in order to execute it.

Mental flexibility therefore means searching and bundling information and experiences on certain topics within milliseconds in these extensive organic neural networks, which cannot be compared with a computer.

Mental flexibility generates understanding, promotes creativity and is important for learning.

As a result, the neural networks (midpoints) can adapt to life and constantly create new ones.

Because the more immobile the mind and brain, the more one reacts like an automaton: new things are put into old drawers; and one keeps running after their information without incorporating the new.
But this would be important in order to create new solutions to a problem or to be able to deal with the world and oneself better, more appropriately and to gain further insights.

So, the more rigid the brain, the less one thinks and reacts - limited by a midpoint - often inappropriately and spontaneously.

So the human mind, driven by unconscious or conscious aims, seeks information in order to carry it out (consciously, if one pays attention to it).

It can appear suddenly, reappear elsewhere, etc.

A good example of mental activity is thinking:

This always means concentrating on a topic, an aim, and what comes to mind in response to the questions posed by the brain – its huge organic networks.

This is caused by an internal or external impulse (from the sensors) that stimulates midpoints in the brain, which in turn activate the attention or consciousness to deal with the appropriate topic (questions, decisions, judgments, etc.). deal with, i.e. to obtain further (inner) information with the mind.

This process of thinking: impulse > midpoints > consciousness > mind > midpoints go on until you have a coherent feeling, you can't get any further or it is replaced by another topic.

Flexibility also means that you don't always accept quick reviews like this, but rather take a closer look at them if they are important to you.

In other words, you should look twice more so that consciousness (better: the sensors) is activated and sends information to the brain, with the aim that synapses (which are responsible for learning) can possibly change.

So, if you create an aim that takes into account the above, you can become more flexible, i.e., include other midpoints, experiences, similarities.

General definition:

"Ghosts" can generally be called targets. Such as zeitgeist (goals that were current at a time) or the humanities, all of which have the goal of finding out something about their category that cannot be scientifically defined precisely - for example due to the complexity.

What was one asked (from philoso-phers):

▶ How does the mind get into the machine (here: the human body)?

Reply:

▶ It does not come into the "machine", but belongs to the brain from the moment it is created and is adequately expanded for its development.

Mind and brain are mutually dependent in humans.
There is no one without the other!

Anyone who claims this anyway (such as Descartes) drives a wedge into the natural interrelationship and opens the floodgates to misinterpretations regarding the psyche.

Minds are structures that are formed by aims.

The more consciousness (with his senses) is activated, the better you can recognize the world and yourself and give the brain the opportunity to learn - to form new aims or midpoints.

The faster midpoints can change, i.e., the better they learn and interact with other midpoints, the more adaptable and flexible the brain is in reaching aims.

The flexibility of the mind depends on the disposition, what has been learned in the course of life and the current condition of the person.

One more remark about the "mind": A mind, in the sense of an immaterial being, which our ancestors felt internally and then projected outwards, because the functioning of the brain - also with regard to the central mechanism - was completely unknown to them, only exists in humans. Everything else is projections that have no substance in reality.

Emotional Sensation

(Definition and Description)

Since the emergence of the first organisms around 3.5 billion years ago, feelings have accompanied life and especially survival.

Feelings arise in humans - like cognitive experiences - due to goals in the brain and are stored in the respective neural networks.

They guide people. In addition to cognition, feeling is the other pillar that controls people.

Everything that a person has experienced or has experienced is accompanied by feelings that are stored.

This means that people's feelings very often play a more dominant role than their cognition.

As I said: Emotions are formed because of goals. They range from fine-tuning (to do something precisely) to violent urges (when the brain judges it to be of the utmost importance) and are often stronger than reason; it's hard to resist them - as everyone knows. They can blind you completely.

The midpoints create a world aligned with the target. This generates corresponding feelings that more or less urge to satisfy the goal. Feelings are therefore dependent on the goals in the brain.

If you have wrong goals in yourself, wrong, mostly unhealthy feelings are also generated.

Feelings can control people very well. Therefore, everything he does, experiences etc. is accompanied by it.

It is much more economical to summarize important situations in feelings, which should later help in similar states to evaluate them more quickly than if the brain were to store all the details of what was in front of a person and act on the basis of this image.

Many variable feelings can overlap and form a pattern that has the character of a request in similar situations.

Regarding wrong goals: In daily life one is dependent on one's cognitions. These show us the world through the goals in the brain. This then also affects the feelings as a result: They are not properly attuned to the world with regard to wrong goals. if e.g. For example, if your gut feeling says you should decide this or that one way or the other, then you can often register later that you made the wrong decision.

Like starting a war with other people.

But the feelings are often right. So, it's not that easy to spot false feelings. But if something very important is at stake, then it would be good to review what has been said above and turn on the thinking. At the same time, this activates the awareness that what the feelings want can be looked at more closely with strengthened senses. And this gives the brain information from its feelings and thinking and thus the possibility to revise its decision.

Again, and again you experience feelings that tell you 100% that this or that is absolutely right and in order and want to lead you there - sometimes with strong urges. However, if you are not an expert in the field (but also sometimes if you are an expert), you should perhaps question these feelings critically. Because the less you know about something, the more your feelings can creatively fool you.

The brain makes its own, sometimes erroneous, interpretations, thereby misleading humans.

Depending on the value of the goal, feelings can be very strong. Especially when an essential value has to be given up. For example, when you're grieving. Here an old goal has to give way to a new one, namely the realization that something you loved is no longer there. The old goal creates the tears, the pain because it can no longer be reached.

So, when you're sad, going through the range of emotions, it's always because of an aim that can no longer be reached. This works until you come to terms with it.

How to perceive the world

(Definition and explanation)

Immediately after conception, feelings take over – and only give them up again with death

One can look at the world as a fixed entity that is the same from every point of view.
This is called outside-in theory.

However, one can also see the world in such a way that different creatures see it differently in terms of their aims.
This is what I call the

inside-out theory.

There, as here, the sensors
receive stimuli from the
outside world. A few impulses are enough to get an
idea.

In contrast to the outside-
in theory, however, the
world is created by the respective living beings according to their goals:
The sensors send the recorded information to the neural
networks. If it is deter-
mined there that the world
they perceive differs from
that stored in the mid-
points, they may process
their view of the world.

This process can be followed immediately:

The world that living be-ings, including humans, per-ceive is one that results from **their aims that neural networks have built up.** (Just as after conception the body builds itself ac-cording to inherited aims, so does the psyche: **these aims create neural networks** in order to be reached.)

According to these, the sen-sors see the world. As soon as the inner world differs from the outer world, the neural networks may change their structures.

This is how man perceives
the world according to his
psychic aims.

**!! The world that shows itself
to us is of course there first,
but what people absorb from
it is decided by the brain according to its aims. !!**

Even if you want to record everything
that is around you, it always remains a
matter of the limits of our senses and
brain.

*Wikipedia (definition): In living beings,
perception is the process and the subjective result of information acquisition
(reception) and processing of stimuli
from the environment and from the
body. This happens through unconscious (and sometimes conscious in
humans) filtering and merging of partial information into subjectively
meaningful overall impressions. These
are also called precepts and are con-
tinuously compared with stored ideas
(constructs and schemes).*

► According to this definition, there would be the world first, which is created by filtering and merging partial information into subjectively meaningful overall impressions in living beings.

This raises the question: According to which directives are the filtering and merging of partial information carried out?

The answer could only be: Through the aims in the brain, which are focused by means of the sensors, which are focused by its values (aims) (i.e. where the attention should be directed).

► So, I think it's the other way around: that first the brain (the midpoints) has an approximate expectation about the world according to its aims. Then this is perceived by the senses selected in this way. Once this is done, inequalities in these two worlds (expec-

tation and fact) are corrected by the brain in milliseconds when it feels right according to its aims.

First of all, you always see the world according to your habits, expectations, and ideas that are stored in your brain about aims. If it recognizes (because it is valuable) that it deviates from it, then the perception is adjusted accordingly. Aims learn or form a new – again initially according to the aims that one has inherited or learned, because only through them can one originally perceive the world.

There is no world as it actually and always is, but only one from the perspective of the respective observer.

Therefore, we do not see the world as it appears to be in front of us (that is, the same for everyone), but one that the brain shows us based on its aims.

Since every person has their own characteristic aims, they also see their own world, to which they react indi-vidually.

(By the way, since each species has its specific goals, the world sees them similarly).

Again: People can only perceive the world from the perspective of the respective observer.

For clarification:

The world that we see is of course still there, even if we are no longer there. However, it would change according to the respective perception by other beings who are different from us.

Because there is no such thing as a world that is always the same.

What stays forever - no matter what perspective you look at it from - is that <u>identical sub-</u>

stances under identical conditions always show identical results.

Summarized:

Human beings see the world
from their point of view. This
results from the aims of the respective person. Namely from
his currently active ones or especially from those currently
additionally stimulated.

▶ The active aims shape the
world into a structure that is
needed to achieve them.

▶ Depending on the value of
the stimuli that are now activated, further aims are awak-
ened, which additionally structure the view.

▶ So, there is ultimately no
identical world that everyone
sees the same, but many dif-

ferent, from the point of view of the respective aims.

And: intellect means to perceive something precisely, i.e. to understand it. You can only grasp what you have a system for.

(If one encounters something absolutely new, then of course one can also take in and grasp it - but, as I said, only according to one's predispositions aims). In this way, the new from the environment and inner field of the human being, from the brain, becomes his predispositions adjusted accordingly.

So, you absorb the world first through the aims in yourself and then with the aligned senses – in that order.

The senses are constantly confronted with unfiltered stimuli (approx. 11 million bits per second), but they do not simply represent the world in front of us 1:1, but the brain selects them with its aims, which align the senses in such a way that they only perceive the information that fits the aims

of the brain because it is important.

These million bits are not there to depict the environment precisely for us, but to compare the structures that arise after selection through our aims with those stored in the brain and, if necessary, to correct them by learning (changing synapses).

In general, then, man has his hereditary world in the head brain, the autonomic nervous system (plus the somatic nervous system) and the abdominal brain (enteric nervous system), along with those who have experiences and learning were built in him.

This is the reason why we each perceive the world differently and possibly wrongly; because we weren't in the right midpoints. (Wrong in relation hung that we have disadvantages, e.g., not respond appropriately.)

And since the selection by the aims also influences the storage of experiences in the brain, this can lead to incorrect information.

A little excursion to objectivity:

How do animals, bacteria and viruses perceive the world?

And who sees the world more correctly?

Of course, people will say: the world ultimately looks the way we see it.

Anyone who says you can only see the world from a human perspective is definitely **right**.

Anyone who believes that this is being said about a basic world that is eternal and unchangeable is certainly **wrong**.

Because the world is basically **not** in an eternally identical state (because processes are constantly taking place on all levels).

A little incentive to think:

What should the brain also perceive when you say you see it for what it is?

The answer is only possible in relation to aims that reside in oneself - in the brain.

And: people's perception is limited. As for hearing and seeing with the respective bandwidth. Or e.g., the inability to perceive radioactivity, magnetism, ultrasound, etc.

There is no world that is the same and unchangeable from every perspective.

Summarized:

Viewed from living beings, the world is subjective.

Recorded by an apparatus - regardless of the perspective - it is always objective.

But this does not mean: forever fixed and immutable, because the world is constantly changing.

Only the laws according to which substances move are eternal.

And all perspectives of the macro- or micro world result in the sentences:

> **● Identical substances under identical circumstances always give identical results.**
> **● The reason for this is that everything is subject to unchangeable laws.**
> **● If you change substances or circumstances, then other laws also appear.**

If you turn 180 degrees in a strange environment, it takes milliseconds before you consciously perceive what is in front of you.

This attaches to the brain: First, the general perception occurs according to its expectations. (If there are no specific ones, it looks for similarities). Depending on the extent to which this does not match what is in front of you, it is corrected if it is relevant.

The aim of orientation requires data from the senses to clarify whether and to what extent the world shown by the brain may deviate from reality in order to be able to adapt. This takes milliseconds. (The aim of orientation is a central aim in living beings).

Recognition also takes place through aims; one recognizes what was stored in the brain. This is also where the reason for confusion can be found (because the brain searches for similarities).

The selected stimuli may change existing neuronal networks in the brain or generate new ones if aims (midpoints) in the psyche consider this to be important. If the stimuli show more or less strong differences from what has been stored up to now, it is adjusted.

By means of the senses, which send information to the brain via attention, this is always up to date - if the aims of perception are not restricted too much by certain (rigid) midpoints.

Without new information from the senses, the brain is virtually blind - and only acts according to the previous information it had stored - as happens in a dream.

First you see the world that you last saved in yourself. If the

senses recognize this differently, the storage changes - if the
brain decides, this is important.

> E.g., when a landscape that
has been seen fleetingly but
assessed as irrelevant is seen
by the senses. (The brain stays
with its vision). <

> It is different when, for ex-
ample, you wake up from sleep
and the world saved before going to bed has changed. At first
you see - expected - the world
after the routine storage. But if
the senses send other stimuli,
then the brain will include them
in its vision, because it is usually important in order to be able
to deal with the immediate
world.
The evaluation and any change
take place very quickly (as I
said: in milliseconds). <

> This is also how it happens in
dreams: the senses, which are
directed inward due to sleep,
take the stimuli of the dream

> **world as facts that the brain - and consequently we - take as reality due to its changed structure during sleep. <**

Regarding knowledge, individual things are not important. It all depends on the aim. If this is to look at details, only then will these be particularly perceived. But when it comes to saving the overall impression, then you perceive it as a whole.

The perception of music can serve as an example: You perceive the whole and not the individual instruments, because that is not the aim. (The whole thing is to perceive the feeling of music). The perception of individual devices would cloud the perception, because it could lead to other central points and be distracted.

This is exactly how you absorb everything in daily life from your goals. And that's how you see the world.

If something is no longer correct (e.g., something dangerous appears) then a target is activated in order to perceive it specifically. This suddenly puts you in a different focus. This is also rec-

orded holistically and creates a different pattern in the brain.

Again: How and with what a room is
filled is initially not important as long
as one is aiming to perceive this room.
Only when you look more closely
through other aims do they gain value.

Conclusion: the brain always absorbs
holistically. The stimulated aims can
change the topics quickly.

THE SELF

The SELF is a relatively small, but - in terms of its values - an essential part in the human brain - and also acts from this.

Among other things, it decides through control efforts with - over its respective midpoints, which have formed from its aims.

It is initially formed from feelings: what I like, what I don't like. Over time, this changes to: I want that, I don't want that. And the SELF forms itself accordingly. The aims are correspondingly stored in the brain and work unconsciously or consciously.

Depending on the level of development, they are supplemented with cognitive personal aims.

That SELF can control areas of the psyche up to certain

**limit thresholds and, if necessary, influence them more or less with his will. So overcome other goals in his psyche via the midpoint-mechanics.
But the stronger other feelings (as goals) are, the more difficult it becomes.
In general: The more the feelings have power in the goals, the more difficult it is for the mind.
This has to be explained - not feelings! These run according to the laws inherent in them, which can make it difficult for the mind to influence.**

This will also have to do with the fact that people have developed through feelings in the course of their evolution - the mind only much later.
Also for this reason - and because it is much easier than us-

ing the mind - feeling is often preferred.

> **The SELF is also a postulated instance in Freud's psychoanalysis, which is equated with consciousness.**
>
> **Now, however, consciousness is merely a function that is intended to provide the goals in the brain with more precise information with increased senses, since they can make adequate decisions.**
>
> **Therefore, Freud's abovementioned ego invention makes no sense.**
>
> # In one sentence: consciousness is not the self!

The SELF, that is, what you mean, what you are yourself, as I said, is formed from the feelings of human being, from his mental state. The beginning is around the end of the 2nd year of life.

Here personal aims gradually emerge.

One more word about the SELF-ideal:

This is how you would like to be your-self. And, as you might think, others should see you.

It can harm you by setting wrong goals.

A few words about

Consciousness

(Explanation)

<u>Consciousness is a term from philosophy that could never be defined precisely and therefore always remained vague.</u>

The reason for this is that philosophers generally did not want to accept that life arose from matter; that it naturally also follows substances and laws.

They want to see in humans a being that, beyond the material, has metaphysical states, experiences and free will, especially with its 'consciousness'.

These are wishes that cannot be fulfilled with the facts, with reality - but are possible with the midpoint - mechanism. In other words: this blind them; thus, fulfils their illusions.

A clear, real definition of consciousness is obtained when it is described with **increased attention** (the function of which is to look at something more closely). This avoids the subliminal reference to metaphysics.

<u>On the one hand</u>, consciousness arises through increased perception with the senses (the sensors*) when certain thresholds are exceeded. Of course, these also immediately activate

all affected neural networks in order to be able to react.

<u>On the other hand</u>, what you do consciously - the knowledge - (far more than 90% happens unconsciously).

This awareness (as concentration) is also only possible through increased perception with the sensors.

(*Inner Sensors are for recording of environmental stimuli and body states and their forwarding.)

The function of consciousness is to take a closer look at something.

Due to a lack of information, consciousness alone cannot make a decision. Even the human mind (as an information seeker in the neuron networks) can only contribute partial information through its activities.

Ultimately, decisions are: concerted results from many neural networks to achieve aims.

The belief that we control ourselves with our consciousness is hardly questioned because the feeling forces this on us with apparent evidence.

This is how we usually experience ourselves as a person in whom consciousness makes all decisions.

The brain is viewed as an aid: as a carrier of memory. In addition, it is recognized that inherited systems and skills are stored here.

It is often less clear that it also regulates all feelings, thinking, speaking, etc.

Because if you take a closer look, it can be realized that the brain directs us, in which the SELF (i.e., its aims) is also located. This is an essential participant and decision maker.

(For normal, daily life, however, it is usually irrelevant to know that the brain controls you: you act and react to what is important for you.)

But it is interesting for everyone who wants to know **why** there is consciousness:

1. The brain shows us the world according to its aims. (It is well known that it selects the world).
2. Consciousness sees them in this form plus what the senses then absorb.
3. It sends this modified image back to the brain. If this decides it is important, increased attention is generated in the senses.
4. These then shows us the world that may have changed as a result of the information.
5. Consciousness now sees them in this form plus what the senses are now absorbing.
6. It sends this information back to the brain.

and so on.

These sequences are repeated every millisecond. Depending on the value, with normal attention or with increased senses (consciousness).

So: **what you z. B. sees is initially made exclusively by the brain, which shows it to us on the basis of its aims.** Then what is experienced by the sensors is sent to the brain, which processes it. And then, depending on the deviation, shows the consciousness a corrected view.

Therefore, consciousness only becomes aware of its milliseconds after the brain has decided.

Because the brain always decides because it has innumerable information in it. Consciousness never decides because it is only experienced and very limited in what the senses can simultaneously absorb from the brain.

Appropriate decisions can only be made with sufficient information.

It follows very clearly from this: *consciousness* or normal attention cannot interpret the world suffi-

ciently for decisions, because this is the domain of the brain; it does not have the information that was more or less stored.

The *brain* cannot experience the present clearly enough, it needs this information from the con-sciousness (the senses) in order to possibly correct its interpretation of the world and decide differently.

The senses (awareness, attention, subliminal absorption) experience through the stimuli.

This experience is then absorbed in the brain - if it has value for the brain - and processed.

Of course, awareness does not decide. The brain makes decisions based on the information and aims it contains.

The SELF decides with - about its respective midpoints.

If it does not get current information, it can of course only judge what is in it.

Ultimately, it's about perception. Either the normal one, which is more general (like moving through a familiar environment). Or an attentive, conscious one, by strengthening the senses (e.g., when you are in an unknown area).

Perception therefore has the task of giving information to the brain through experience. This may generate new learning processes, make corrections, change settings, activate aims, etc.

The brain creates suggestions, anticipates them, anticipates results – consciousness experiences and transmits the resulting perspectives and information back to the brain.

If something is currently important to us, something dangerous, unusual or new occurs, decisions or activities of the neuronal networks cross a certain threshold in the brain, it strengthens our senses. As a result, one perceives the outside and inside world more intensely and consciously. You experience them more vividly.

The intensified senses, i.e., the consciousness, then send the recorded information to the brain – especially to the neuronal networks affected by it, which (largely with their feelings) may make a change in the assessment and attitude. This result is perceived again, etc.

If the brain ultimately decides against the feeling, you can get a bad gut feeling. This arises because the aim, the decision, is not carried out in a different but similar situation, which intensifies the gut feeling.

It is the nature of the aims: If an aim is not achieved, then it is emotionally compelling to pursue it further.

Appendix: Definition of Thought

> Thinking is a process that searches within itself - starting from the thinker's goals (his midpoints, i.e. neural networks) - to get answers to questions.

Everything that man has inherited and experienced can be found here – in whatever form.

This results in the loop: question > answer > question again > answer etc.

Dreams

Why they are so strange

I would like to send in advance:

In general, it is assumed - without reflection - that we perceive the world with our consciousness and thus also decide.

→ *We do not understand the course of the dream event (which we value as a reality in sleep) when we are awake. Because we view the outside world that we see as a fixed reality.*

Only when we recognize that our brain - more precisely: the neural networks - first shows us the world and then immediately afterwards the information of the senses from the outside world is processed (if it deviates from the stored one) it is clear that the world is not a fixed reality, but can only be seen from one perspective.

For the dreams this means: Since we perceive the world through our brain while we are awake and evaluate it as reality, we also do the same with the dreams while we are asleep. ←

This clarifies some questions:

Why do we take in the world like this?

▶ *Science knows that we select them.*

According to which directives?

▶ *According to our aims.*

Where are these located?

►*In the brain -* ***and not in the consciousness!***

It follows from this: We do not see the world as it "actually" is, but as it is best used to us from the perspective of the brain.

Now the world is constantly changing. This leads to the question: How do we get new information?

►*By the senses. In this way, consciousness takes in the world and sends it to the brain.*

This can then change its aims. With the result that we then see the world differently.

**Consciousness is in-
creased perception
through the senses -
nothing else!**

It absorbs information from outside and from inside the person.

When you sleep, it is usually only from the inside (except for a few external stimuli that have overcome the now higher thresholds), which, as usual, it sends to the brain.

▶The brain works differently during sleep because it lacks the abilities of the frontal lobe (including its logical accompaniment). Various network connections also change.

This means that the cerebral cortex, which is responsible for the logical viewing of events, loses this function during sleep. As a result, somewhat bizarre impressions appear real.

And since it is now receiving different information, other is-

**sues arise for it to
see the world by.**

**And so, the brain shows us a
world in sleep, which we value
as reality through our senses,
which we perceive from within.**

The fact that the dream event is so incomprehensible after we have woken up again is explained by the now no longer restricted perceptual ability of the outside world, including the frontal lobe: the senses can again absorb all information that the aims of the brain allow.

From this point of view, what happens in the dream then makes no sense.

Dream world and the world that we see with a fully functioning brain are therefore very different and, as I said, generate what the senses send to the brain (and what we then perceive).

Understanding these perceptions causes difficulties for people who continue to live in the perspective of their usual world.

But even experts have their seemingly insurmountable (especially emotional) problems to see that it is not the consciousness that carries out and decides everything, but the brain.

So, the perception of our dreams, which we grasp as absolute reality, remains **an unsolvable puzzle** for them.

In dreams, feelings have power.

The mind is mostly off.

Any thought (when awake again) that something metaphysical was involved is just wishful thinking.

In contrast to being awake, where aims of adaptation with the cere-

brum dominate, dreams are about topics of the respective living being that are no longer influenced by the midpoints. The cerebrum, among other things, does not play a role here because it has largely been shut down. This is how the fantasies of dreams are perceived as reality.

Sleep is about <u>recovery from wakefulness</u>, in which one can constantly be brought back from the midpoint into structures.

In the dream it is about the continued working of the senses, which are now directed inwards. Since a number of functions of the brain have been shut down, they show topics and processes that are not geared towards a final result - like the aims (although here, too, only substances run according to laws).

You shouldn't take your dreams so seriously. They are surreal stimuli, scenes or stories that arise through associations, similarities, etc. Overall, however, they have little to do with reality.

You can see this, for example, in day-dreams that are triggered by any kind of impulses, similarities, and generate fantasies.

Of course, this would not be seen as reality either.

Of course, this can of course also include wishes, fears, desires, fears, etc. of oneself, which have been stimulated.

Not infrequently it is somehow stimulated emotions that are experienced unbridled as reality with vivid fantasies.

Although the dream, like everything else, consists of substances that operate according to laws, it is of little use in life as a prophet, because everything is mixed up, realities do not matter.

This is mostly due to the similarities that are no longer monitored e.g., by the midpoints, especially in which the frontal lobe plays a major role.

Whether we are awake or asleep; our brain is always working. And absorbs information from the outside and inside world with the senses:

► **When we are awake**, primarily from the outside world in order to be able to adapt. This changes and adjusts the aims in the brain and, of course, at the same time the midpoints that execute them. While awake, the midpoints often sort out what does not fit their aims (including fantasies, illogical, dreams). Through this mechanism, the senses then no longer noticed.

► **In sleep** from the inner world, because this is precisely the task of the senses. Here, the aims with their midpoints are not active (also because, as I said, they would interfere with recovery during sleep). The brain is not ruled from the midpoints. But about topics that jumble up what is currently being stimulated.

The brain works similarly in dreams and in wakefulness. Except that in the latter, the midpoints are in charge, showing the whole direction.

And during sleep brain functions are restricted.

In both cases we experience the world - and it appears real to us.

Aims are geared toward a final state.

Topics don't – they are open.

All topics can of course become aims while being awake - if they have ex-ceeded certain thresholds - and then play an active part in the psyche.

To repeat it again:

In the dream, the brain shows us how it works in itself, unregulated by the midpoint mechanics of being awake, among other things by restricting the frontal lobe and the striated muscles during sleep. This is why dreams are often so incomprehensible (see above). They show us, in relation to reality, a restricted world through the senses.

Since certain functions are disabled during sleep, issues can arise that are not perceived while awake. Here, aims can also play a role that are no longer excluded from midpoints because there is often no space for them.

This can also include fantasies that came into our heads while we were awake, but classified as irrelevant or nonsensical - but were still saved.

Of course, problems, conflicts or wishes, etc. are also stimulated in the dream, which are then "processed". The results are mostly fantasies, unrealistic "solutions."

Or not, as in the case of traumatic experiences, the causes of which are evoked during sleep and can turn into nightmares.

It can show the most bizarre stories and images that we take as absolute reality - until we are again awake and everyday cognitive behaviour, including the frontal lobe function, has taken over again.

We are used to living purposefully, to bring everything in an understandable direction. And so, the dream is also interpreted accordingly. It is assumed to have an inner stringency - which is certainly incorrect.

Dreaming while sleeping just tells us how the brain works without the aims of wakefulness. As a rule, it does not depict how we should act (because it only has limited functions). And it especially doesn't show us how metaphysical, God, or supernatural wants to move us to do something.

You should keep in mind that the brain - like everything - consists of substances that operate according to laws.

Question: Why did it not occur to people in the past that dreams are exclusively produced by their brain?

Answer: Because they did not know how the brain works and that it is exclusively what shapes them. And remained in their belief in metaphysical activities because they couldn't explain it to themselves otherwise.

It's always like this: If something is not clear to you, then interpretations, interpretations, fantasies come into play. These fill in the "knowledge hole". And so, people have often looked for the origin of their dreams in the outside world, for example given by God or other mystical instructions.

If you ask yourself what dreams are supposed to show us, the answer is:

They tell us little that is useful. Because this is not their job.

But by thinking about your interpretation of dreams while awake, you could learn something about yourself - which aims and problems, among others, shape us.

That also means what the psyche is unconsciously busy with.

Conclusion:

• We sleep because it helps us recover from the waking state.

• We dream because our senses always remain active (if only to be able to absorb dangers from the environment).

Brain vs. Computer

To anticipate: the brain is a self-organizing structure based on its aims.

The computer is a commodity designed by humans for computing power.

And:

Man's world is as his aims show him to be.

The computer world is as its programmers designed it.

The brain has the task of ensuring human survival; it is always active.

The computer has to perform arithmetic tasks that man has given up (with algorithms - a rule created in the language of the computer - which consists of a precise sequence of instructions with which certain tasks can be carried out in a given time to be done). To do this, it only has to be active until the work is done.

Calculation speed plays a secondary role for the brain; The connections of the neuron networks have priority.

The brain is a tissue that works according to organic laws - the computer is a calculator created from inorganic parts that needs specifications and cannot be creative by itself. Although it can calculate much faster than a brain, it lacks the creative element that enables creative solutions through endless linking possibilities:

Because the fact that the brain is busy with something, associations are very often stimulated: similarities. Often just any place you've been to and had a similar thought or feeling is enough.

If one wanted to build a computer that could be as creative as the human brain, this would probably be simply impossible: the computer would have to be infinitely flexible and be able to change its structure again and again at lightning speed. Not only information itself, but also all associations to it must be able to be linked. And this every time new information arrives.

That would be impossible for a machine whose basic substance is computing power. *Only biological substances like brains can do that.*

An essential control mechanism of human beings are feelings, which i.e., be generated by the brain.

It is not possible for a computer to generate feelings - similar to a human being.

The brain is there to form a structure according to the respective aims. These aims have been in the brain since time immemorial, or they are always new after they have been procreated.

Everything in the brain can be influenced by everything. This must not be in the computer because otherwise he will not be able to carry out his bills - he will no longer be able to carry out his work step by step. He needs clear commands about what should be involved.

The central aim of the brain is that the living thing survives - adapts itself as possible to the environment. For this purpose, there are always various networks of neurons active in the brain that can constantly change their value flexibly.

The central aim of the computer is to calculate each time after the programming.

The brain carries out countless tasks at the same time and the priorities can change constantly - the computer is clearly overburdened here. It can only process a fraction of what the brain can do - and if so, then only with much more energy than the brain.

Many processes in the brain always run in parallel and new ones are constantly being added. There are always new synapses (which are responsible for learning) that strengthen or recede.

Processing steps in the computer can also be carried out in parallel. But nowhere near the size of the brain.

The computer needs clear relationships *- the brain draws conclusions from facts and (sometimes diffuse) information from outside and inside.*

This makes it possible for the brain to be creative. A computer cannot do that - for the reasons mentioned.

The brain is able to learn for a lifetime because it has to adapt to changing circumstances over and over again. This is not always the case, but is usually better for survival, because it can change flexibly again.

The brain is always active - the computer only when information arrives. *The brain never sleeps because it has to be careful about whether life is threatened – like a bird that is constantly on the lookout for danger.*

What can a person think of when naming the word red? Unprecedented associations, such as love experiences, traffic accidents, the setting sun, blood, colours of autumn, the cloth in the bullring, colour of flags, blast furnaces, etc.

What does the computer show when you enter red? A limited number of answers that humans have programmed once. There are only references (links) but no automatic associations (unless man links them). Feelings that are very strongly activated by the word red, for example, are lost on the computer because it is numb. This is an important advantage for humans because feelings are among other things fine control elements that are important for reacting and acting.

In this example - and no matter what word or concept it is - you can also see the difference between the brain and the computer very well.

The computer is a machine built by humans, the aim of which is to calculate. It does not use components that have nothing to do with each other - that do not fit into its strict logic-based calculation.

For example, a captcha - randomly arranged numbers and letters - are relatively easy to read for humans, with their similarity approach, but for computers this is virtually impossible because letters and numbers are so distorted that their systems cannot read them.

A computer needs commands to work step by step. *The brain acts on its own and creates new goals time and again, only by driving the survival and well-being of the living being.*

A computer almost never makes mistakes because it only calculates logically.

The brain can make a number of mistakes because it is creative and can draw wrong conclusions. The advantage, however, is the tremendous flexibility that allows you to use all components and networks for the respective goals with your mind. The downside is that it wants to explain everything and often does not look closely. The advantage is that it can produce results that often make sense from a nebulous occurrence from a few clues.

The computer always makes rational decisions - the brain can make irrational decisions that can make sense for each aim.

So, as you can see on closer inspection, they are two very different systems.

If one reads in general about the comparison brain - computer, then it is

noticeable that time and again the speed is mentioned.
This does not play the central role in the brain in this regard, but the link; That's the way man lives. And that does not create in this form and to this extent a computer - also not approximately.

People are always learning, forming new synapses and neural networks. Whenever someone has learned something, new synapses have formed or been amplified in his brain.

On the other hand, these are restricted or deleted when they are no longer used.

The individual synapses, which are available in billions of times, can each connect thousands of times with other synapses.

To reproduce all this into a computer, and let it act just like the brain, is hardly possible.

Conclusion: The brain is an organic tissue that wants to survive with humans and uses all the similarities in it. It makes its own interpretation, imag-

es and "truths". It always creates new aims.

The computer runs according to exactly predetermined steps.

Both are subject to precise but different laws. These are two completely different systems, each of which can only be described individually.

And a few more words about artificial intelligence (AI):

Intelligence means using it to find the most satisfactory solutions and answers to questions and problems. This usually involves a topic.

Humans cannot store as much information as AI - in terms of the

> potentially huge amount of information stored - because the brain only has a limited cognitive memory. It acquires memories of this through similarities with the task at hand, which are collected via feelings.

If you ask what pure intelligence is, the answer is: everything that is not accompanied by feelings.

This is alien to humans, because both sides (cognition and feelings) usually play a role in them.

The AI is supposed to suggest answers. To do this, it searches through all the data that could be part of the solution.

In this way, AI can give a satisfactory answer based on a precisely defined question.

And artificial intelligence (with its algorithms) answer questions that are sought in the stored information.

The brain (with its mind located within it for searching) and artificial intelligence (with its algorithms) answer questions that are sought in the stored information. As living tissue, the brain stores these primarily with feelings and cognitively. This is because life wants to preserve itself. And feelings (with regard to storage) have proven to be a space-saving option in the course of evolution.

AI, as a structure without feelings, does not have this aim; it only stores the information "cognitively". This allows it to answer questions that do not require sensory perceptions for answers (although it can of course add corresponding intelligent information about living beings that experience them).

The advantage over life is that feelings cannot distort the answers. For example, if answers do not fit for ethical reasons or personal views.

In general, when a person asks himself something, he not only receives cognitive answers from himself, but also emotional ones. These often take precedence and influence the result.

This is not the case with AI - of course it cannot, because it has no feelings.

If all information relating to a particular topic is stored and then the question arises as to how this can be used for a task and what suggestions there are, then AI has a clear advantage, as long as it does not involve emotions. Because it can store much more useful data and information than the brain, which usually also responds emotionally and thus possibly waters down the sober answer - but provides creative (emotional) answers.

- **Life began about 3.5 billion years ago from matter - together with the emergence of feelings. With extensions, it still prefers to use them to make judgments today.**
- **Artificial intelligence forms answers from facts - uninfluenced by feelings.**

> "CP" represents countless conver-
> sations partner with whom I have
> discussed the topics for many
> years.

Part 2 conversations

Aims page 110

Laws page 141

Coincidence page 162

Midpoint-mechanics page 187

How the brain works page 205

Attitude towards life with the concept of yin and yang page 215

Epilogue page 219

Foreword

The central error that people make out of ignorance to this day is to believe that their species does <u>not</u>, like everything else in the universe, run exclusively according to aims that are subject to laws.

One believes to be something extraordinary, to occupy a special position.

Although educated people (due to their midpoint) are likely to dismiss it, this behaviour can very clearly be characterized as <u>hubris</u>.

The consequence of this attitude is that people have difficulties in ultimately understanding themselves.

And: That his brain shows him everything possible through his

midpoint for reasons of self-esteem in order to maintain this belief (as an aim).

But if you realize that people also act completely according to the law, then of course that doesn't mean that you no longer have a love of life. His aims are still there. If they are reached, he has a good feeling.

But what then (if you acknowledge it) no longer works is belief (as an aim) in something supernatural, metaphysical.

So, I assume that everything in the universe – including humans – is subject to laws.

> **And: Everything has the aim of forming a structure according to the laws.**

It follows:

> **1. Identical substances under identical circumstances always give identical results.**
>
> **2. The reason for this is that everything is subject to unchangeable laws.**
>
> **3. If you change substances or circumstances, then other laws also appear.**

Conversation about

The central im-portance of aims

With the topic:
Gestalt Psychology
Universal scholar
Consciousness Restriction
Thinking habits
Life Attitudes
Fear of death
Thirst for knowledge

If you want to know yourself, ask about your aims.

The most important point is their nature: if they are not met, they urge (more or less), depending on the current or general value in a feeling self, somehow to be

reached after all - even with alternatives.

"Aims (often synonymous with values) consist of networks of neurons, synapses and glial cells. These act as a knitting pattern and mark or generate a way there when activated. In this way they structure – via midpoints – the brain and, in direct succession, the people and the world."

"You say that all living beings are aligned with aims. How did you come up to this? "*CP* was curious.

"I was wondering why people do what they do. And have observed time and time again that aims (as midpoints) shape people - as long as they are in the waking state of attention. "

"And outside of wakefulness?"

"When you are asleep, or similar states where the midpoints have diminished in their activity, and the brain structure changes drastically. For example, the work of the frontal lobe is significantly redesigned.

The difference between to be awake and sleep is that in the former the midpoints provide structure; The frontal lobe has a significant share in the aims sought here. Whereas they are partially reduced to zero during sleep (the forehead brain is then partially blocked - such as the logical functions). So, the midpoints have little influence on the brain, which can therefore conjure up the strangest images.

Not infrequently it is somehow stimulated emotions that are experienced unbridled as reality with vivid fantasies.

So, other mechanisms and laws are active.

Of course, everything continues to run according to substances and laws - only according to other, for example, biochemical aims."

"How do you define 'aims'?"

"General: **Form a structure that leads to the desired endpoint of a path. For this, two things are needed: First, man must form a structure in himself and he must see the world in a structure that shows a suitable path. And that's how all living things do it, because their original purpose is to survival. "**

"That means that the living being structures itself, takes itself into a different shape?" asked CP.

"No, the respective aim is this form".

"Aims are very important in your theory building," stated CP.

"In fact, everything is structured by it," I nodded. "Take the system of life.

In every living being, there is a spectrum of aims that relativize, detach, connect with each other, form co-operative groups, cover up, wrestle for supremacy, and organize themselves into a partially alternate hierarchy. Aims are added, others change or go out. Each target has, or generates, its opponent, if other targets are touched and run the risk of being compromised. And every action takes place through a set of aims that each develop structures, compromise, reinforce or weaken. Many aims change in the course of life, except for the very low-lying, for example, the life instinct. This one always remains, even if you are very old."

"That sounds very complicated," said CP.

"It is, too," I nodded again. "The whole system is incredibly diverse and nested. That makes it so difficult to tell exactly where the driving forces of action come from.

Every behaviour, if traced back, will have its source in the life instinct. There are usually many intermediate stages between this and the current behaviour. That's why it's often hard to find the connections. But the younger a living being, the easier it is to determine. In the course of his life man differentiates more and more. It builds up increasingly, depending on the aims it carries. "

"Can you never get to the bottom of the psyche?"

"Not in the smallest detail. But if you want to try to recognize yourself, it helps to know that everything is designed in one of midpoints - like the aims of the SELF, which are in the brain and play an important role.

Ultimately, people are always circling around the same aims, only the content is different. The highest aim is, as a rule, the life instinct, which, it seems, always wants to grow, wants more and higher, closely followed by the aim of orientation, showing people his environment, which is of value to them, in positive or negative Meaning, in order to be able to react accordingly. The most important design factor is then the group - starting with two people - the society in which one lives.

The aim of being recognized is probably one of the strongest things that shapes you in life. In this way, the society in which one lives can become totally one's own world. That is, they can talk about their goals, in other words: values that, among other things, were anchored by the socialization process, shape them absolutely and do not allow other goals to have a chance."

"You say there's no life without a midpoint?"

"Let me redefine what I mean by 'midpoint': it means the world that is created to reach an aim. Everything else is more or less shielded. He selects from what he finds and believes he has a value for the aim, and gives shape to the world. Imagine the unimaginable: completely without aims. In you, the aim would no longer be to survive, to satisfy your needs, to orient oneself. From the very beginning of the first life in the world, you would find the aim of survival, which created the 'sight' and brought the found world into a form.

A strong aim can completely take over the human being for a period of time and structure it completely. This can be seen very well in the phenomenon of love, or when you have a task in front of you that completely engages you. Everything in one is aligned as much as possible."

"You meant the aims in man are hierarchical. Are you saying that there is a command center in the brain?"

"No, this does not exist. What I mean by this is that the more important the aims are, the higher the rank. To achieve this, neural networks join together to form jointly acting groups, ensembles. The hierarchy can change constantly according to the demands of the world."

"When and how did these networks actually come about?"

"Human brain development begins in the third week of pregnancy and is largely complete only 20 to 30 years after birth.

At the time of birth, the infant already has almost the entire number of neurons, but only a very small part of the nerve processes, i.e. synapses. These then multiply at breathtaking speed and network the neurons.

They are then amplified or dissipate again."

"By what rules?"

"According to the respective aims. It depends on what value they have and how intensively they are used. Experiences with the environment determine which neural networks become stronger, endure and which do not."

"So the decisive factors are the experiences that the living being makes in the various phases?"

"Heredity also plays an important role in neural networks. Plant and environmental estimates assume that both contribute roughly half each. Which distribution they unite in detail depends on the respective aims.

The more important something is for a living being, the more it learns in this relationship. Neural networks are strengthened, reshaped, regenerate or die out."

"Do the individual neurons only react to a specific impulse?"

"No, they can form structures for different impulses with different neurons, they have a multiple function, so to speak: For the respective aims, many nerve cells have the possibility, in milliseconds, of an impulse with other cells, which have an equal potential in themselves to organize.

Take about a life-threatening situation. This structure over various activated neurons lightnings fast your shape. The more life, the survival is affected, the stronger the activities. "

"So, no order is given from 'above'?"

"The 'command' is the perception, the impulse, which is then translated into reactions - if there is an aim for it, and the impulse has the corresponding valence."

"What determines the valence?"

"The aims that lie in one."

"But if you say that the life instinct is usually at the top of the hierarchy,

then it would have to be found somewhere!"

"It lies in the primordial structures of
living beings that have passed it on
through DNA."

"Could one define the goals in humans
as neuron associations, which e.g.
stimulated by stimuli to form a structure?"

"Yes. And in the same way that neurons can have multiple functions, so
too are the individual aims: They can
organize themselves into groups – into
goals that can form forms of action.
Various goals are then always stimulated in parallel, which together form
structures."

"Let me repeat: the impulse, the stim-
ulus from outside or inside activates
aims, these activate further neural
networks and these again solution
programs."

"That's the procedure," I confirmed.

"When you go from one midpoint to
the other, is it like switching from one
neural network to another?"

"Yes."

"Once again asked: Everything is subject to aims?"

"Yes, whether inorganic or organic."

"So not just the living beings?"

"Look: After the big bang there was mostly hydrogen, helium and some lithium and beryllium. From these gases galaxies with solar systems and planets developed under great pressures, and all the elements we know today formed during this time. All this was inorganic until a certain point in time. "

"And was shaped based on aims?"

"When substances or their environment are changed, different forms and laws result. **Everything has the aim of forming a figure according to the laws.** Exactly that is also subject to everything organic. What they all have in common is that they are guided by aims. From this perspective, there is no difference between the inanimate and the animated. With the latter, 'only' the aims of survival are added, which have led to ever more complex structures.'

"Why do you often not see that aims shape you?"

"Quite simply because you believe you are shaping yourself with your consciousness."

--- Gestalt psychology ---

After a break, *CP* continued.

"You certainly know **Max Wertheimer**, who said: 'There are relationships in which not everything that happens as a whole derives from the way the individual pieces are and are composed, but conversely, where - in a pertinent case - what, what in a part of this whole happens, determined by internal structural laws of this its whole. '"

I nodded. "These inner structural laws result from aims in the human being; they absorb what he is receptive to, what is important to him and store this as a whole. This is e.g. when listening to music, of course, the melody and not the individual instruments.

This holistic view is an important property of all living beings."

"Wertheimer's Gestalt theory, then, seeks to clarify the laws by which the brain joins elements into a whole," concluded *CP*.

"These are explained neither by the laws of the individual parts nor by their sum," I added. "But they are explained by the respective aim in the human being, which brings all parts with its midpoint into a structure appropriate to the aim, which is then stored in the brain.

Holistic recognition makes sense to handle situations better and faster. "

"I'll recap," GP said. "The holistic view of the brain has the aim of being able to make quick decisions – if it went into all the details every time, this would delay its understanding or decision-making. This holistic view arises in people through experiences that they have already had in similar situations. However, since these are only similar, it does not necessarily mean that they are appropriate in relation to this goal, or that it correctly interprets what lies in front of it.

"Right. This usually results in a structure that you can work with without getting bogged down in the details."

--- Universal scholar ---

"And you say everything in the universe is shaped by aims," GP continued to be curious.

"Everything has the aim to form a figure according to the respective laws. Everything is aligned with aims. "

"Even a lifeless stone?" CP smiled.

"By 'lifeless stone' you probably mean something lying around somewhere. Well, I would like to say: First, there is movement within the stone, because it consists of atoms or even smaller particle waves, which are not motionless and also run according to laws. And secondly, when this stone is moved, then it forms with its environment, the circumstances of a particular structure according to the laws. That's what I mean when I say: everything has the aim of forming a figure according to the laws."

"Could a stone form a structure even without laws?"

"How come? This is impossible because the laws are inherent in the substances. Nothing can happen without laws, because the substances are laws! "

"And so, you came to the conclusion that everything has the aim of forming a figure according to the laws."

"Right, this happens completely automatically. It is not that a stone has a consciousness that is out to obtain information. It's not alive. But since, as

I said, everything runs according to laws, the aim automatically arises to create structures according to the laws of nature.

The same thing happens to the living beings, except that here the aim of survival is added. This aim shapes the human being. This is what I call midpoint or midpoint-mechanics.

Imagine a person who has no more aims. So do not eat anymore, drink, etc. What would happen to that? "

"He would probably die."

"By the way: without an aim, the placebo effect wouldn't work either. The aim here is to achieve something through medication. This creates a midpoint that pulls in everything that is useful for that aim. Of course, also experiences that were made when you were already taking any medication that helped. The logic of the brain is: If a suitable drug, which comes from a competent person, is taken against this disease, then this aim will also be fulfilled.

As a result, the previous internal structure in this relationship can change up to the fulfilment of the aim: from illness to health."

"And this is done by the brain just because it "recognized" a drug that helps in his view?"

"Yes, that is enough. Unless, for example, the consciousness (better: the perception of the senses) gives the information that there is no active ingredient in the drug or that one does not trust the person who prescribed it. This would severely limit or negate the effect.

--- Consciousness restriction ---

The vast majority of human reactions are unaware. Consciousness becomes only a very small part, and always when something important occurs. Then information about the consciousness is obtained. If they are relevant, the brain processes them with the midpoints.

All other reactions and behaviours occur through general attention.

Attention wanders; absorbs the outer and inner world with the senses more loosely.

(This is the basic principle of all life: to learn particularly information about dangers and food resources).

Awareness, i.e. increased attention, deals with something in a targeted manner.

"But that must be an incredible amount of aims with their midpoints that shape the people!"

"Yes, you can say that. Just such a simple act as picking up a newspaper requires many learned aims that have been summarized and then run automatically.

Time and again, I hear that people have trouble understanding that everything is guided by aims, including themselves. I think its daily life that makes them fail to understand that sentence. Because everything is so natural, what happens. If they dig deeper, then they could see that every action, every movement is guided by aims and moves them. For example, the handle to the glass of water and drink from it. "

"Many people I've talked to actually have trouble understanding what 'aim' means," *CP* nodded. "For them, one aim is to complete a task or strive for something. But such a simple thing, such as bringing a spoon to your mouth, is not an aim for them!"

"Because it runs automatically, without paying more attention to this process. If they were to get to the bottom of this, they would come closer to the fact that every single hand movement must first be learned. The motivation for this was aims.

Because that's just the treachery for the realization that simple actions are taken for granted and not further think about it. Not realized that very specific aim-oriented processes are behind it."

"Yes, that's right," CP remarked thoughtfully.

"Lots of amazing achievements by people who are often based on island talents, for example to remember a large number of things in a limited time, to perform complex arithmetic operations in a few seconds or to learn a new language in a short time, would not be possible without an aim. This provides the structure that leads to the solution. Even artificial intelligence, which works with algorithms, does not come to a conclusion without a specified aim. "

--- thinking habits ---

I took a short break.

Then I continued: "Until the 16th century, people knew virtually no laws. Everything was determined from God's perspective. But even in our time, many are far from seeing everything controlled by aims, thinking that most things happen by themselves anyway, and still viewing consciousness as something metaphysical or something. These views have passed from generation to generation and still shape some philosophers and people who deal with these issues. Everyone else usually just takes it that way because they do not even think about it. "

"Why don't man often see that aims shape him?"

"Simply because man believe that he shapes himself with his consciousness."

"What if they were to throw their antiquated views overboard and start thinking that consciousness is indeed just a brain information provider?"

"Most people are too caught up in their views, their habits of thinking. In the least, the aim is to get to the bottom of the processes in them, to deal intensively with the course of their consciousness, as with this topic. Added to this there are innumerable people who live in the world of esoteric mysticism and, if they accept this insight, injure their world. For them consciousness is an essential element in the mystical view of the world, which is shaped by a metaphysical aim with its midpoint in them. "

"You mean they create this aim themself? "

"Secure. Without noticing it."

"The truth does not interest them, do you mean to say that," said *CP*.

"They are interested in the truth," I replied, "but only their truth". Everything else is labelled as nonsense.

One can call this the drama of the blinded human being. Its midpoint, the mystical world, surrounds it like a bell shielding all other views and evidence."

"Pity," regretted *CP*, "I find it always very exciting to hear and discuss new views."

"I feel the same way", I nodded. "Unfortunately, it is often the case that each of us has a world view that involves a more or less strong perseverance. Changes to beloved settings are reluctant to make.

For example, branded images and ideas of the culture in which you grew up are transported from generation to generation. Only too rarely are these questioned, and if so, often with bad feelings, because they question the structures they have created: in themselves and in society. Resistance quickly builds up, trying by all means to maintain the old structures. "

"Self-knowledge apparently does not belong to the aims of many people," said *CP*.

"I have that impression too. Self-knowledge comes through self-observation. Who does that?"

"Funny, I enjoy watching myself and sometimes have to laugh heartily when I've seen things wrong or insisted on an erroneous point of view. By introspection, one comes closer, sees moves in ones that have not yet noticed, especially in new or critical situations.

Maybe it's also because I can accept myself and my behaviour, with the sentence, 'What happened, had to happen as it happened.' "

"I feel the same way," I confirmed. "That's why I enjoy talking to you. I've learned a lot from you already. "

"The compliment I can give back, the discussions with you are very stimulating for me.

What aims should one have?", he continued.

"I can't answer that like that. The aim is to dictate something to others, not within me. Everyone has their own values. I can only speak for myself here, for my aims: The most important thing for me is knowledge. I can completely immerse myself in it.

What comes to mind is that dissatisfaction always depends on the level of expectation."

"You mean, the decisive factor is the respective aim?"

"The more you have achieved an aim, the higher the satisfaction - and vice versa. Here you can find roots for euphoria and especially depression.

Therefore, one should think carefully, which aims one undertakes. Are its wrong aims, for example, that cannot be achieved, then you open the door to bad mood or depressions. False aims can severely burden the psyche."

"Do you have ideals?"

"Not really, unless you count the truth."

"Would wealth and fame give you something?"

"If I had the sense of wealth, then I would have to write for the people according to their expectations. So, fairy tales, sex, crime. These would not be desirable aims for me. I am absolutely satisfied with my life, in which I search for new insights. I have nothing of wealth, because what I want to know is primarily in me and rises spontaneously. So, much money would not help me in this respect.

And fame could possibly create vanity in me that does not help my actual aims, but rather hinders them. It could stop me from time to time questioning my theses and possibly insisting on them, even against legitimate objections.

There are enough examples of famous personalities. "

"You are different than most people."

"I did not aspire to that. I am the way
I am, and that's how I take myself. "

"Why do people strive for greatness,
for wanting to have more and more?"

"One reason will be vanity. An essential element of life is the recognition in
the group, the society. The general
reasons will lie in the primordial structures. "

"Therefore, people are striving for
wealth, build taller buildings, clothe
themselves conspicuously, show what
they have, try to achieve a high position in society?"

"I think that's the driving force. Many
people are shaped by this. "

--- fear of death ---

"Are you afraid of death?"

"I know that the midpoint of life-drive
creates this fear to drive people to
continue living. For example, it does
not matter to him whether human being is terminally ill and suffers from
136

horrible pain or only wishes to die. Knowing the reason makes it easier for me to deal with these feelings. And: If you're dead, the reason is gone anyway, then feelings logically play no role anymore."

"Why do many people think that death is something very bad?"

"Because the life instinct is fooling everyone. He is the strongest midpoint of life. "

"But in the end, he's just a target."

"Naturally. Therefore, for example, the suicide is also nothing wrong. Anyone who believes this merely reflects his own opinion or that of the society in which he grew up or lives. "

"And the own opinion is always relative," *CP* added.

"What do you think about near-death experiences?" He asked.

"Dying is the extinction of the organ functions of a living being, which leads

137

to death. Death is the function setting of the neural networks in the brain.

Experiences can always only be gained through the brain. And as long as this is not dead, it is capable of producing fantasies. When the brain is dead, you do not experience anything anymore.

Near-death experiences come clearly from the brain. And the brain is not always right with what's coming out of it - that we see very clearly in the dreams."

So, one should not attach great importance to near-death experiences."

--- thirst for knowledge ---

"Can one say, Mr. Hermsch, you are always on the trail of yourself?"

"That's not quite true, but I often spontaneously have thoughts and feelings that I follow, with which I study intensively. I research, compare, falsify and verify and try, if they help me in my desire to understand, finally to bring them understandable on paper. Hoping to get criticized if I'm wrong about a view.

In addition, there is a strange striving for perfection in the relationship that I want to answer questions that are in me to the smallest detail. These aims are sustainable in me, so even if I have answered questions, they pop up again and again and make me check to see if my answer was correct or had any errors. "

"From uncertainty?"

"Out of openness and the pursuit of perfection."

"So, it's not just the urge for an answer that makes you think of something, it's the urge for it?"

"Through this quest for perfection fall to me answers. And since these aims are sustainable in me, there seems to be no end to it. That's why criticism is important to me. And that's why I write.

In addition, dealing with a question always raises new questions. So, my urge to learn never actually comes to a conclusion.

Even while falling asleep, there are suddenly thoughts or ideas, for example, about topics that I had once occupied myself with, but where I had no solution.

I then take notes for a moment, because I had the experience that if I did not write it down right away, the thoughts would have disappeared the next day. A voluntary retrieval of these target solutions is not possible for me after I wake up again. "

"All this seems to give you a lot," presumed *CP*.

"I can be completely absorbed in it", I confirmed.

Laws are immanent and unchangeable.

(Conversation about)

With the topic:
- Causality
- Probability calculation
- Chaos
- Physical Laws and God?
- Meaning of life only through reli-
gion?
- Acceptance of nature
- Rules of good and evil

---

1. Identical substances under identical circumstances always give identical results.

2. The reason for this is that everything is subject to unchangeable laws.

3. If you change substances or circumstances, then other laws also appear.

That also means: There are no substances without laws.

No one can separate or change them. The formula: substances = laws is universal.

CP remarked: "Your definition of 'laws' is: Identical parts or waves in identical circumstances always result in identical structures."

I nodded.

"Is there something that is identical?" he asked sceptically.

"That's a good question. I have therefore formulated the sentence in such a way that it is unambiguous and well-defined.

As a rule, I express it in a modified form: the more similar substances and circumstances are, the more similar are the structures or laws resulting from them.

But back to your question: I would describe 'identical' like this: A substance - with or without mass - that matches all of its properties with another. It follows that both operate according to identical laws.

If 'identical substances under identical circumstances' did not achieve an identical result, then either the substances or the circumstances were not identical.

"Is there anything in the content of the universe that does not follow the law?"

"No, laws are inherent in everything.

That's why not everything is possible, only what the laws allow."

"You also claim that all laws are eternal," CP continued.

"That's right, the same substances in the same circumstances always result in the same thing. You can never change a law. However, as soon as you subtract or add something from a substance, other laws arise.

The Gestalt theory is suitable as an example. She says that the essence of something can only be grasped from its entirety, not if it is reduced to the individual pieces that make it up. From the totality, which ultimately always creates the brain (and thus adds something), a new lawfulness and view of the human being results."

Where do the laws come from, who made them?" CP continued to research.

"Nobody made them, just as nobody created the universe. As I said, they are inherent in the substances."

There are no substances without laws.

"So, the laws are in the substances and the respective environment," CP thought out loud.

"Anyone can check that," I nodded. "The same things - or substances - in the same circumstances always result in the same. It is a universal law.

This is valid in the macro world as well as in the micro world, the world of the smallest particle waves. The only difference is that the micro-world is more susceptible to influences, such as interactions, and the laws here are more difficult to determine. "

"Why did only a few people notice that **everything** went according to the law?" CP asked thoughtfully.

"Because the world is constantly in motion. This movement incessantly creates new constellations, each of which runs according to different laws.

It would not be important for survival to realize that everything is done according to the law. It is important to react appropriately to changes. Therefore, there was no aim to check exactly whether the same substances always achieve the same result under the same circumstances - which is the definition of the law.

But anyone who tries to refute this sentence will conclude that it cannot be refuted."

--- causality ---

"What about the causality?", *CP* was still curious. "It says, that every effect has a cause."

"This is valid in the macro world as well as in the micro world, the world of quanta. In the macro world we live in, this is obvious if you look for the cause long enough.

In the microworld this is not immediately clear. Since it is much more difficult to measure or observe in the quantum world without interfering with the process, it is very often the case that coincidence occurs here. (I call coincidence ignorance of the legal process). Here, of course, causality is also present because the inherent laws of elementary parts and the local or non-local environment are the cause of the effects. That's how they build their structures. "

"So, the problem is not," concluded *CP*, "that in the quantum world, not everything works according to laws, but that one can observe and measure them much more difficult. So, you're dealing with a measurement or observation problem in general? "

"The word 'coincidence' is often used for this," I nodded. "Today, interaction-free quantum measurement can be used to measure very well.

Here comes a particular phrase that should not be forgotten: 'Everything has the aim of forming a structure according to the laws.' If you look for it, quantum mechanics loses the mystery and you take it for granted."

"How could one imagine elementary particles, such as an electron that is simultaneously wave and particle?" He was curious.

"Many elementary particles are subject to this fact. We are used to introducing ourselves to one or the other, for example in quick succession. Imagining a part in two exactly opposite properties at the same time is not possible for us, for example, to think of a cat as dead and alive at the same time.

An aid can be the yin and yang symbol. This is meant to express those opposing properties are one. When immersed in it, this image dissolves into a non-objective cloud. Such a cloud is also the reality of the elementary particles. "

"Atoms are made up of elementary particles, such as electrons, protons, neutrons, (and smaller elements, such as quarks, leptons, etc.), that is, virtu-al clouds," *CP* considered.

"Yes, atoms and their components are clouds, in which particles and wave form a unit. They run according to their inherent laws that determine when they fall apart.

That man cannot make predictions by observing or measuring the decay of an atom should be clear from what has just been said. Perhaps one can still imagine the virtual clouds, but then also recognizing the respective laws according to which they run is virtually impossible. "

"Well, just because we cannot make a precise prediction about the decay of an atom, and then conclude that something is happening out of nothing, has no basis whatsoever," concluded *CP*.

--- probability calculation ---

"That's clear," I agreed. "The particle-wave clouds are unimaginative to hu-mans about the exact process. They are, as I said, neither exactly to meas-ure nor to observe. Unless you try the

148

math. Because this can make very accurate predictions with the probability calculus.

But that is only possible because everything is legal. And because the number of possible variations in a system is very diverse, but finite.

That's why not everything is possible.

Albert Einstein once said, 'How can mathematics, after all a product of human thought, regardless of experience, really match the realities?'

My Answer: Because the real thing is governed by laws. And because the particular set of structures involved in this relationship is limited.

This is to be understood, because mathematical probability calculus otherwise could make no clear statements.

--- Chaos ---

"They say chaos, meaning complete disorder," *CP* commented. "You say, even in chaos, everything goes according to laws?"

"With the disorder, do you mean that predictions about the course are not possible?" I asked back.

"Yes," *CP* nodded.

"And when predictions are impossible, then disorder prevails?" I prodded.

"That's the way it is said."

"Well, in chaos move parts or particles, waves. Why should not this process be legal? "

"As I said, predictions about the course are not possible."

"It's the same knitting pattern as what we just discussed," I shook my head. "Because you cannot predict something, it is concluded that there are no laws, and we use the word coincidence. Is not that too easy? Because 'structure' can of course also mean 'disorder'. In this case, 'goal' simply means that processes are carried out according to laws and not that the parts form into a certain order according to the human imagination.

CP considered. "True," he said then, "it has yet to be proven. In fact, the chaotic behaviour we see is no proof that there are no laws here. "

I nodded. "Chaos also means the unpredictability due to the initial state of a system. For example, if you take two seemingly absolutely equal initial states under the same circumstances and the prediction for the outcome is different, then you have not accounted for exactly all the components that played a role in the initial state, or others, that flowed in during the process."

"That would mean that everything is determined even in chaos, but not all components were known or taken into account," CP reflected.

"The opinion that not everything is done according to substances and laws, but is in this respect like fast. Out of ignorance and because we cannot dive into the chaos inside to see it closely. Not infrequently, to prove something mystical.

This scheme is used whenever it is difficult for a person to take a deeper look at what is happening. Like the dream, which often seems completely incomprehensible. "

"But it still runs according to the law?" CP assured himself again.

"For sure. Neurons work according to laws.

But you quickly reach its limits if you want to make concrete statements.

--- Physical laws and God? ---

How else than by law should the substances in the universe run out? "

"Well," replied *CP*, "there are people who say, by the hand of God."

"Well, can you imagine that, for example, physical laws can be changed by a hand movement of God or no longer apply?"

"Not really."

"People who say that are not serious in my view. They live in their world, in their midpoints and these simply exclude the facts, the reality with their complexes. Thus, man escapes reality."

"But they also argue: Can my feeling be wrong, that tells me with absolute certainty that God exists? Can my feelings tell me something wrong? "

"There is a clear answer to that: of course. If you look closely at his own behaviour, the question will answer itself. How often have people been deceived by their feelings?

By the way," I added, "laws in this sense were not known before the 17th century. Everything was ordained by God for the people living at that time."

"But after that," wondered *CP*, "it became more and more clear what role the laws play."

"Laws have the connotation of compulsion. People do not like compulsion. They prefer to believe that they decide to have their freedom. This is not conducive to the truth, but to their faith.

And then there are the cultural traditions that have carried on the belief in God from generation to generation. That was also gladly accepted, among other things, because it could temporarily escape the harsh reality. "

-- Meaning of life only through religion? --

"It is said religions are meaningful," *CP* interjected.

"Well, if you look at the history of religions, then you can conclude that they are nonsensical, to say the least moderately."

"But where should man get the meaning of his life? And what I always wanted to ask: what exactly does sense mean? "

"Travel, walk, take a direction. So, meaning is the aim.

Regarding the question of the meaning of life: You can help other people, you can stand up for tolerance, you can lead a self-determined life for your most important aims, etc. In any case, these aims are laid out in people in their primordial structures. Mirror neurons, which I call mirror-midpoints, are activated. One sees or interprets the other, this stimulates similarities which again stimulate central points in one. This way one can feel similarly, empathize. You don't need a religion to react in a human way, for example to help.

If you then look at the justifications given by the religions for their existence! And what atrocities people have already done to others through religious belief.

It is only people who have created the religions and who have then enforced other people according to their own, sometimes very selfish aims.

If one translates meaning with aim and looks at what religions have done, then one can only be warned against this 'meaningfulness'. "

"But what about the hold that faith gives people and from which they can draw strength?" added CP.

"That's another thing. This has nothing more to do with the external reality, but exclusively with the interior of man. There is no question that faith, as the midpoint, can help people to better face mental conflicts."

"But is not it too sober when you say everything is legal?" *CP* still came to mind.

"Since all substances are inseparable from laws, you should just take it that way. Look around the world at how colourful she is: people with their be-haviours and ideas, nature in all its manifestations. Of course, everything works according to laws. Is that really only sober to call? "

--- Acceptance of nature ---

"It occurs to me," *CP* changed the sub-ject, "is the fact that everything works according to laws, for the people, for the society to accept at all?"

"That's a good question. You could have asked: Do people like the bare truth? "

"So, the truth you're standing for," *CP* noted.

"Everyone has the opportunity to refute my truth or to find one's own.

I believe, following my truth, that one would then stand between the acceptance of reality and its own midpoints. For the aims in man, in society, of course, want to be realized. This is the truth in the way and it is probably rather ignored, because otherwise the aims would seem to be impossible to achieve.

For example, if someone stole something, it is understandable from the point of view that everything had to happen the way it did, but it does not fit with the values, aims of the people who demand punishment and retribution. "

"How could one unite these fundamental opposites?"

"Through tolerance and insight, on the one hand, saying it had to happen that way, and on the other hand, our rules are important to us. You could argue, "If you get off scot-free now, our rules would be in jeopardy. And more importantly, this would apply not just to this case, but eventually over time.

157

That could lead to internal tensions in society.

This tension can only be resolved by judging, 'You have broken a rule that applies to all of us, including you, and that is why you must be punished.

It's true that everything had to happen the way it did, but a society would break apart if you accepted everything and let everything go. Because it is held together by rules. "

--- Rules of good and evil ---

"Where do these rules come from?"

"The ideas of good and evil are formed unconsciously or consciously, unwritten or written, for example through the primordial structures in the human being, a cultural imprint, as aims in each group or society. These assessments then act more or less in the form of social norms and moral concepts in every member of society. "

"You mean," summed up *CP*, "who did something that harmed others, and believes he does not have to take responsibility for it, because: what had

158

to happen, how it happened, should be remembered has violated the rules or laws of a group or society that would not be viable in the long run without them.

Because the opinion that others represent, their judgment, of course had to be done as it happened. Therefore, the offender cannot blame the judges for the verdict.

With the sentence: 'Everything's going according to laws', it should only be shown that everything had to happen the way it happened. "

"You have reproduced that well," I agreed.

"So, as far as possible, elements of understanding should be taken into account when assessing the sentence and should be included in the judgment," added *CP*.

"Yes, but most people will hardly worry about it because they just want to stay in their midpoints, and such insights are obstacles. So, they will have little understanding of the wrongdoing of other people (wrongdoing in terms of the aims of society). "

"But a big plus to the attitude that everything is predetermined," stated *CP*, "is that you can come to terms with what happened in the past more quickly."

"That's true," I agreed. "It's even a huge gain, because it makes you live more in the present and is less shaped by the past.

For example, the anger that breaks out in some people when they have not reached their aim is not very meaningful in view of what we have just discussed.

This is especially true for mistakes we make. So, if we curse ourselves, it can be particularly destabilizing for one's self. "

"But humanly understandable," he interjected.

"You're right.

Another advantage of the attitude that everything had to happen as it was is the tolerance that comes from the sentence and can have a positive effect on yourself and living together with other people.

One more word about the punishments that people pronounce against others: A deed is usually judged by the degree to which one was hurt in one's feelings. These feelings, it is demanded, should also be compensated by the judges by punishment. "

Conversation about

Coincidence and its legitimate reasons

Coincidence does not come out of nowhere and always has its legal reasons.

With the topics:
Ignorance
Objective coincidence
Information
Computer
Determinism
Mysticism
Meditations

"I noticed," said CP, "that the word 'coincidence' is often used."

"Coincidence is a synonym for 'not knowing'", I explained. "When some-one talks about it, they mean something that occurred unexpectedly, that could not be calculated or predicted.

If you look closely, you will notice that the word 'coincidence' actually often means 'without cause or reason' or even more drastic; 'something that has fallen out of nowhere' is used.

These examples are often used to argue for the just mentioned coincidence out of thin air.

And more 'arguments':

• One speaks of coincidence when no causal explanation can be found for a single event or the coincidence of several events.

• Radioactive decay is not a deterministic process. The decay time of the individual atomic nucleus is absolutely random.

• Chance directs the microcosm. In the atomic world, individual events are fundamentally no longer precisely predictable (no longer deterministic).

Comment from me: Many statements can be discovered in the

same or similar form ('no causal explanation can be found').

Hardly anyone takes into account **that there are exact laws in every substance**, which lead to the respective "random" events and are of course causal. "

"Why not?"

"Because it is impossible for humans to know all laws in every substance.

If something is there, it is always substance and law at the same time:

> **1. Identical substances under identical circumstances always give identical results.**
>
> **2. The reason for this is that everything is subject to unchangeable laws.**
>
> **3. If you change substances or circumstances, then other laws also appear.**

In order to make statements about events anyway, one prefers to fall back on 'causal reasons' (but does not mean laws, but components) and says, if one does not find any, these events are random.

('Causal reason' is valid as proof of an uninterrupted chain of components that have produced something, or to be able to use them to predict a result.)

This type of observation in the macroscopic area was created and was successful.

And unfortunately, after the discoveries in microscopic space – especially with regard to quantum physics – it was transferred to it.

Here, however, due to complicated or impossible measurements, causal chains are ultimately more difficult or not to prove.

And that's why the word 'coincidence' is often used here.

However, as explained above, laws work in all substances, be it in the macro or microscopic area.

So, the question is: does one have to represent causal chains of elements in order to prove determinism?

Or is it not much more precise to show the laws that move the substances or to assume that everything is shaped by them.

Because everything has the aim of forming a structure according to the laws.

There are two points of view here:

- Something arises from nothing.
- Everything has a reason.

I am convinced of the latter. "

--- ignorance ---

CP nodded. "So, the word is basically used for ignorance of the legal processes".

"That's the way it is." You can generally add to coincidence: ... because I don't know the legal processes that led to it.

Because all substances in the universe (which of course also include the quantum) run according to laws.

Therefore, everything is determined.

But if one wanted to prove the determinateness of causal chains for predictions, one would quickly fail – because the amount of substances and laws go beyond all human dimensions.

This is how all substances work according to laws: An identical substance under an identical environment always gives an identical result.

The fact that one could get into difficulties in producing particles with an identical environment in the quantum world does not refute this thesis.

If they are modified in the form: The same substances under the same conditions always give the same result, then these difficulties could be avoided.

"Could it be put on this guideline?" asked CP.

'Coincident is a synonym for igno-rance of legal processes that are not exactly known'.

"I can agree to that immediately," I nodded.

--- objective coincidence ---

"Now there are quantum physicists who speak of the 'objective coinci-dence'", CP thought. "They mean that if you do an experiment in the world of elementary particles in which two identical particles, different in time, do not achieve identical results under identical circumstances, that there are no hidden variables that could be said to be this unequal have triggered the result. "

"As we have already established: coin-cident is synonymous with ignorance. **You have no way of knowing how many local or non-local influences have had an effect on the respec-tive particles temporarily present here, all of which have their own laws.** (Law also means that particles always show identical results due to identical interaction.)

Because, and this is the proof that everything also works in quantum systems according to laws: with statistical probability calculation, very precise predictions can be made in quantum systems. It would be impossible if there was lawlessness here. "

"Could you say that the hidden variables that are mentioned again and again are in the respective laws?" asked CP.

"It hits the nail on the head," I confirmed.

Humans, if they want to know something exactly, are also dependent on measurements in quantum systems.

If this is not possible – for example using the Heisenberg uncertainty principle – then only the path of the mathematical description remains.

But then you can make very precise statements for quantum systems.

Of course, this is only possible because here, as everywhere, everything is done according to laws.

For objective coincidence:

"Objective" means that something without human influence (such as measurement or perspective) is what it is at the moment. If a coincidence comes into play here (something that has fallen to the legal object, for example due to the inner constellation), then this is, so to speak, an objective coincidence.

An objective event always has a legitimate reason.

When people say that something is impossible to measure by them, it does not prove that there are no laws here.

This also applies to the objection that statistical probability does not include everything 100 percent and is therefore proof that not everything is done according to the law."

"A really weak argument," CP nodded.

A brief comment on the Heisenberg uncertainty principle (Wikipedia):

When measuring x-coordinate and x-impulse, their order must be determined, and in precisely these cases the second measurement changes the state created by the first measurement once more. Therefore, a subsequent repetition of the first measurement would now have a different result. So it's possible that two observables, acting on a state in different orders, can deliver different final states.

--- information ---

And: There are quantum physicists who claim that quantum needs information in order to 'know' what to do.

But inorganic doesn't need any information. The substances run naturally according to the laws.

Inorganic matter only needs information if people want to use it to achieve an aim – not per se, because it works according to substances and laws anyway and it doesn't matter what happens.

(By the way: if you inform something (and they work) you change a legal process.)

On the other hand, it is different with living things: Since they do not know the future, but have to decide on the right ways to reach their aims, they need information, for example, to save their lives.

As I said, this is no more the case with inorganic matter in the macro world than in the micro world e.g., the quanta, molecules, atoms. It doesn't matter what happens here. "

So, whoever claims that inorganic needs information is wrong.

(By the way: it would be better to speak of laws than of information.)

Because, as I said, inorganic substances do not need information; they consist of laws.

So, if you want to recognize a substance, you would have to observe its laws, which it follows.

"I repeat again," said CP. "So, you can say that individual elementary particles do not carry any information. Therefore, they cannot give us any information. They run according to the laws of their wholeness (with the environment).

It can therefore be said that identical elementary particles always achieve identical results under identical environments.

If this does not result, then either the elementary particles or the environment was not identical. "

"Exactly," I nodded.

--- computer ---

"What I can think of right now, "meant CP," Computers also need information!"

"That's right, computers are devices that need information by means of human input in order to know which data they should process and with which method."

"What is the difference between the brain and the computer?"

"An example of this is Captcha, a test on the Internet that shows whether an application is being used by a person or a computer. They are graphically represented, alienated letters and numbers that you have to recognize during the registration process and have to enter in a query window.

The human being with his ability to be creative, to draw conclusions from similarities, succeeds in a few moments. A computer fails because it calculates rigidly and cannot translate infinitely ambiguous parts of images precisely.

The computer has a binary structure, it works on the basis of zeros and ones. He has a rigid (arithmetic) specification.

The brain has a creative structure that is open to all similarities. Creativity means connecting similarities that occur in a wide variety of areas. In some way, everything resembles something else: such as colour, size, temporal proximity, physical proximity, geometric shape, faces, etc. This list could be continued for a long time. And so, there are no limits to creativity.

That is why it is particularly creative during sleep, because here the mid-point of the day's events does not intervene.

By the way: these similarities are also the reason for confusion. Just like a source for brilliant insights. "

"So, creativity is not something super-natural," added CP, "but takes place in people based on aims."

"Right," I nodded. "In addition, the brain is constantly creative, it makes what we perceive fluid, that is, it makes everything out of a 'good' shape that is easy to deal with. So, the aim here is not to analyse the situation down to the smallest detail, but to present it in such a way that you can quickly get an idea of it – and that is the real reason – to survive better.

This also includes the 'creativity of the moment'. This is particularly active in discussions or when you are dealing with something more intensively. It means that something new suddenly appears in you that fits the topic well."

"So, the brain usually simplifies," CP concluded.

"Right. Because no living being in the world could find its way and survive, that would break down every situation into its individual parts at any time. That is also the reason why people experience the world to look in its entirety. "

The computer software can be observed and measured. This is hardly possible in the quantum world.

So, one should not humanize the elementary particles in the sense that they need information. Every world has its own laws. So, everything has to happen as it is, and so everything is predetermined by law. And there is no mysticism that many people like to project into it."

--- determinism ---

"What about determinism?" CP was now curious.

"There are two opposing worldviews: **determinism and indeterminism** (as already indicated above).

Determinism says that everything in the universe has its reasons, according to the laws.

The other group believes that a lot is happening for no reason. Here are a few examples:

- Events happen without cause
- comes out of nowhere
- that there is free will
- there is a metaphysical power behind it.

As I said, I belong to the first group. Because I believe that nothing can happen out of nowhere. "

"You mean, in the end it is essential that everything in the universe proceeds according to laws and that every event is therefore predetermined."

"It's clear to me.

"It is also said that you for example cannot predict the decay of a radioactive atom: exactly when it will happen," continued CP.

"We've spoken about this before, that is precisely determined by the inherent laws and the local or non-local environment.

A substance, here an atom, is internally something that is constantly in motion. The laws always change accordingly. Because the structure changes, and every structural change creates different laws. It already follows that the decay of a radioactive atom cannot be predicted exactly.

And a substance in the quantum world (which happens according to laws) is hardly ever isolated. It always has a local and non-local environment, which legally determines the course.

It is not enough just to look at the particle itself, you have to factor in the surroundings, which makes it extremely difficult to recognize.

"You want to say: If you limit something, then you exclude something."

"Yes, boundaries are always drawn arbitrarily. It is human nature. He has to deal with substances that he can count on to come to a result, for example to be able to act."

"What are the causes, where exactly do these demarcations come from that people make?"

"From the midpoints-mechanics. The midpoints select what suits the aim. "

"Limits are drawn through the midpoints."

"If you included all irrelevant facts in our world, you would be unable to act."

"You can't do that anyway, because the amount would be immeasurably large," CP concluded.

"Yes, and that's why it makes sense to draw boundaries in the macroscopic area of action."

--- mysticism ---

"Since we also mentioned mysticism," chimed in GP, "how could one explain phenomena like 'Chi'?"

"By wishing and believing in it.

E.g. to learn a worldview.

Here you can see the effect of the midpoint principle: you set an aim. Through concentration and practice, a neural network is formed that comes ever closer to this aim, be it inner calm, contemplation with a 'higher' being, martial arts, etc. – to perfection. The human being is subtly structured down to the last detail.

Of course, other aims lose more and more value during the exercise and can therefore affect the course less.

Chi is not something supernatural, but can be practiced and learned through a focus, which usually takes a long time.

This attitude will have an impact on everyday life, because even here you may perceive unwanted thoughts and feelings, but respond less to them. And here, too, you can achieve the aims that are active in you with more energy.

This is especially true for breath-yoga. This has a holistic effect on the general psyche of humans via neuron networks.

Likewise, if people want to believe in higher beings, such as a god. The midpoints of contemplation especially include the primal-structures (in which the 'essence of God' originated). It also allows the experiences that the brain has given the child in the magical phase.

There are many people who have never heard of the magic phase. In other words, the experiences, images and feelings that they experienced during their childhood mostly continue to work in them completely unconsciously. "

"Anyway, I know that," CP nodded.

-- meditations --

"And how about the mindfulness-exercises?" he asked further now.

"'Mindfulness', 'being in the middle of it', 'doing what you do' is about staying with what you are doing, such as resentment to the past or fear of the future, who want to present themselves in thoughts and feelings, especially by weakening or erasing them by becoming the focus of the present.

This happens through the midpoints, similar to chi, which draws attention away from anything else that is not part of it. None of this is something mystical or supersensible, even if the actors would like to see it that way.

Of course, thoughts and feelings keep coming up. In the mindfulness exercises, you should notice them when they are very strong, but do not respond to them, but stick to where you are.

If one would go into this, then these thoughts or feelings form, that is to say midpoints, which shape one, consume energy and thus weaken mindfulness. "

"So, if there is no other way, you should perceive thoughts and feelings," summarized CP, "do not 'suppress' them, but just leave them as they were and continue to be mindful of what you are."

"This is the central purpose of this exercise, so you can completely focus on the respective focus."

"How do you meditate?" CP was curious.

"Let me briefly introduce the course of a meditation: It starts with the aim of switching off all thoughts, feelings and perceptions. So, it is very important to stop the incessant chatter of thoughts. Concentration on this creates brisk neuronal activity in the attention-center of the brain. This signals that the inflow of neuronal information is being slowed down. As a result, an area that is responsible for our orientation in space is increasingly cut off from neuronal impulses. If the area lacks the necessary stimuli, the only thing left is to create the subjective impression of complete spacelessness, which is interpreted as infinite space and eternity. Another area is responsible for imagining the limitations of our body. The total loss of signals on this page means that the perception of yourself becomes limitless. As the depth of meditation increases, the boundary between the inner and outer world blurs and there is a feeling that you are expanding and blending in with the surroundings. Due to the concentration, the flood of information from which people get their orientation disappears. As a result, the boundary between yourself and the world also disappears, the feeling of oneness with the world and limitlessness arises. In the deepest meditation you have the feeling of becoming one with the universe, of dissolving into something much larger."

"That sounds interesting," pondered CP, "does this process happen automatically in the brain when you are at the center of meditation?"

"Yes, if this aim works and you keep practicing.

> **My** meditation practice is that I want to keep getting closer to the end of the universe when I breathe in and to stay directly below this limit that I just reached when I breathe out.
>
> Of course, since the universe is infinite, I can never reach the end of the universe. And so, I can continue this exercise indefinitely.

On this occasion, a word about 're-pression': Imagine that you focus your attention on something that you do not want to admit and respond to it.

This makes this something stronger because pressure creates back pressure. This is how you get into the midpoint of it. With the repression you achieve exactly the opposite of what you want, namely to push something aside. Therefore, you should only perceive it, but then not respond to it."

"But it is also said: 'You repress something' if something continues to act unconsciously."

"It has become commonplace because you believed that you did the repression yourself with your own will and didn't know anything about the midpoints: As a rule, the value of other midpoints is reduced so that it is no longer perceived, but continues to act in the unconscious without the consciousness being able to obtain information."

If you say: 'A midpoint or midpoints do not let you see something', then you hit the facts much more precisely than if someone said: 'You have suppressed something.'

"So, it's always about bringing awareness or attention to an aim," CP continued.

"The emphasis is on one aim," I stressed. "If the aim of forgetting the past were to play an active role, the effect of the first aim would automatically be weakened.

One is, for example, in the 'here and now' when the perception is directed towards the present and this information is sent to the brain. This means that it is less concerned with the past and the future, but primarily with the present."

"So, it's actually always the focus of attention on something that can also be 'nothing'," repeated CP.

"Right, it's about letting go. Just be in the midpoint of the moment. If you are distracted, the sentences 'what happened had to happen how it happened' and 'what will happen will happen how it has to happen' are particularly effective."

Conversation about

Midpoint-mechanics

The midpoint-mechanics is the key to the psyche.

CP and I went for a walk around the lake Alster in Hamburg.

"Why do aims in your scriptures play such a central role?" *CP* wanted to know.

"Well, because they structure every-thing, put it in a shape: **Everything has the aim to form a structure according to the laws.**

Let's take the human being: **The mid-point is the shape that makes an aim out of a person.**

As a general knitting pattern, the example of how to learn to ride a bike:

In the beginning there is the aim. This creates a neural network in the brain to reach it.

Balance, muscles, tendons, posture, mental processes, etc. are developed as sub-goals in the required form, coordinated with one another and temporarily stored.

So gradually the skills are improved; you learn from your mistakes.

This is all done by the neural networks formed by the aim of cycling and then further evolving to expand body-psyche coordination and fine-tune adjustments.

The network at the beginning (the focus of cycling) has now become far-reaching interdependencies. Which, when the respective sub-goals have been achieved, are stored permanently and become an automatic behaviour that is activated when you get back on the bike.

While everything in the universe is shaped by aims that are 'no matter' to the implications of their intended structure, the aim of conservation is added to living beings. These conservation aims are formed in the brain by networks of neurons, which are connected via synapses and which, as I said, I call 'midpoints'.

Depending on the species and individual, the living beings are designed by them.

So, midpoints are made up of neurons distributed far the brain, forming a network that serves to create attitudes, actions, ideas, feelings, and so on. Each midpoint it's an aim that allows for everything that suits to achieve it, paying little or no attention to anything else."

It is very rare for only one midpoint to act; mostly, various are included that are suitable to achieve the goal. "

"Then the midpoint is a key to understanding human beings?"

"Yes - of all living beings. To reach an aim, you have to go one way. If you want to express 'way' more broadly, then you can say: you need a structure. And indeed, the way in the environment must be structured and of course the person who wants to achieve this aim. Everything that could contribute to this structure and is tangible at the moment is taken into account by the aim - everything else remains unused.

For example, if you focus heavily on reaching an aim, you will realize afterwards that he has not noticed anything else. Only what suited his purpose.

One comes closer to oneself each time one recognizes in which midpoint one was."

"I understood it that way," *CP* summarized: "A midpoint wants to be realized. This requires a specific structure. This is created from what is relevant, everything else is disregarded. Should something be disturbing, it is reduced in value, so it can make people much less".

I nodded. "This lowering of the other values does not happen willingly, but mechanically. It is a legal process, that's why I called it 'midpoint-mechanics'."

"It is not deliberately suppressed, but it happens automatically through the midpoint?"

"An example: On March 24, 2015, a pilot in a passenger plane flew into suicide. He steered the plane against a huge rock. He tore all 150 inmates to death.

What happened in the head of this person?"

"He has supplanted everything else," *CP* concluded.

"Imagine that you're focusing your attention on something you do not want to admit. This makes this something stronger because you are dealing with it (you are so in the midpoint of it, you are shaped by it). With repression, you get exactly the opposite of what you want, to put something aside. "

"But it is also said, 'One displaces something when something unconsciously continues to act.'"

"That is also incorrect in the true sense of the word. It is reduced in value from other midpoints so that it is no longer perceived, but can continue to work in the unconscious. – However, not if a current midpoint is very strong.

The answer to what was going on in the co-pilot's head is the midpoint-mechanics: The aim is to take his own life, sat all other midpoints worth reduced or zero - the impending impact of the mountains, the 150 people who were on board and had to die with him, their relatives who suffered the loss, etc.

On the one hand, it's frightening what midpoints can do, such as the incredible atrocities of the Nazi regime or inhumane acts that virtually all nations have perpetrated. "

"Or what individual people did to others," added *CP*.

"Yes. On the other hand, it's nice what midpoints can do. For example, the love to enter for humans or other living beings.

By the way: This also explains the essence of mediation: Here, a midpoint is formed, which becomes stronger with the time and the intensity and amount of the exercises and lowers all other midpoints in value.

As a rule, of course, there is not only one midpoint in the psyche, but many who complement each other, inhibit or only partially play along. They can act together, form mega-nets (clusters), for example, to ensure repetitive processes, integrate into new ones, find themselves together for specific actions.

As adaptation is a central theme for life, new midpoints are always forming.

Here's an example of how midpoints work: People like to argue about whether humans can be altruistic. Surely, he can, because: If he is in the midpoint of helping others, then the midpoints of selfishness, which are actually strong aims in humans, can be eliminated.

However, in the strict sense, there is no selflessness because the aim is to satisfy one's own feelings. "

"What can one do to avoid a midpoint, not to be a slave?"

"Beat him with his own weapons: choose another midpoint or create something new."

"How do you best achieve an aim?"

"By reinforcing the midpoint: paying attention only to what is important to the aim.

If that is not enough, then a new target can be formed that includes more neuron groups, which are automatically selected for how well they might contribute to the solution.

Again, you can see the selection principle of the midpoint.

In addition, similarities in other areas are searched for each aim. Whether there is experience, or by logic, such as the exclusion process, whether solutions are suitable for the problem. And rejects all offered 'solutions' that are illogical in the experience, not fit to achieve this aim or nothing similar to the one to a similarity Theme in common. "

"So, aims are the mainsprings?"

"As often as you investigate, you will always meet aims that have driven, structured the human being.

They can seriously change our perception: through the midpoint-mechanics.

Imagine a tremendous amount of aims that are interconnected. "

"You mean the brain."

"Yes, the neurons that are in contact with each other through the synapses. There are about 100 billion neurons and 100 trillion synapses in the brain. Neurons form networks to perform certain functions.

Everything in the brain runs according to laws. The brain creates the midpoints and these structures the human. "

We sat down on a bench and watched the sailboats cruising the Alster. It was a wonderful day.

"I once wrote a conversation between Peter, a friend of mine, and Phil Osof, which I would like to reproduce here:"

"The midpoint means the world that is created to reach an aim," explained Phil Osof.

"An aim creates a world?"

"To achieve an aim, you need a structure. The midpoint is designed and is this structure. He evaluates the world and the people and puts together what is useful for achieving the aim. Everything else is more or less shielded."

"You think the midpoint is the facts that are interesting for the aim? And brings the people and the world in the appropriate form? "Peter hooked.

"The midpoint is the shape that makes an aim of a human.

He structures the perception of the outer world and of oneself. He chooses what he finds and thinks it has value for the aim. He gives shape to the world. "

"That really sounds like," Peter said, "as if through the midpoint a new world would emerge."

"That's right," Phil Osof nodded. "He's redesigning. This can go so far that you cannot see things as they were, because they are totally re-evaluated.

The midpoint can be like a sorcerer, changing everything with lightning speed. This is how a new world is created. This gives rise to freedom, meaning that one does not perceive much, or only perceives it marginally. At the same time, however, one is also trapped in the midpoint and no longer sees many things. It only comes to the fore, which is important. Everything else goes by, so to speak, suddenly has no value. "

"So, is the midpoint at the same time freedom and prison?" Peter wondered.

"That's the way to express it."

So, "midpoint" is what you call the perceptual world of living beings?" "he wanted to know.

"Yes, the world- and the self-perception. What and how creatures perceive depends on their aims, or in other words: we (our brains) do not simply model the world in ourselves, but create a world of perception based on our aims and the particular spectrum of our senses. The amount of information that comes from the world, but that we ultimately shape ourselves from our human perspective and can only capture within our intake corridors, must be selected. This will get the midpoints. They choose what fits the aims."

"I remember once saying, 'Everything is aligned with aims.'"

Osof nodded again. "Living beings are controlled exclusively by aims. There is nothing that does not originate in it. "

One more question came to Peters mind: "But is not the world actually what it is? How can she be so different and suddenly different?"

"When the aims change, the substances change. Because different substances are needed for each goal. And when they change, the world also changes because it is composed of substances. "

"From the human point of view," I interjected.

"Yes. But ultimately, what we see is always from the point of view of human beings."

"Then there is really no 'world in itself'?", I was curious.

"Yes - of course, the objective world can be depicted using photography, for example, because the subjective influences are not present here at first.

Beyond that, however, there are only views of it from the living beings. Every living entity sees her differently, from what is important to him. And this view shapes his world and himself. The world is not a rigid entity, but a 'something' that can be seen infinitely varied by the living beings. And there are as many worlds as there are living things."

"That would mean that we ourselves make the world that we see through our aims."

"It is exactly like that".

I believe that whoever sees the world can only see it from their own perspective.

As a rule, this is a real human perspective that our brain shows us - so it's not an illusion.

And: The **objective world** can, of course, be depicted by means of photography - because initially the subjective influences are not present here."

"So a camera can depict the world objectively?"

"Yes, depending on the setting (distance, resolution, special perspectives).

But the camera can only take a snapshot with it."

"Still," I shook my head, "I think the world is what it is, and we need to adapt, so shape it."

"Of course," Osof replied.

"But is not that a contradiction?" Peter wondered. "What do you think makes the world or us the world?"

"First of all, our brain shapes the world according to its aims - compares them with what it has holistically stored. When differences arise that it sees with its (enhanced) senses (and these differences have a certain value), then it learns.

Peter considered. "So, we see them according to our values (aims). And since everyone has their own individual aims, those of their group, their country and those of the respective community of values, this is how they see the world. "

"Exactly," nodded Osof.

‼ The world that shows itself to us is there first.

But what a person sees or perceives from this, the brain decides according to its aims.‼

Max Wertheimer says: "There are connections in which not everything that happens as a whole derives from the way in which the individual pieces are composed, but conversely, where - in a pertinent case - what happens in a part of this whole, determined by internal structural laws of this his whole".

When differences occur (and they have a certain value), the midpoints learn.

So, it can also absorb something totally new, if e.g., the aim of life is threatened."

"And we always only see the world that selects our aims, put together?"

"Yes," nodded Phil Osof, "that's how we make the world, we can only see it from a human perspective."

"That was an exhaustive information," *CP* thanked. "How did Phil Osof get to the mechanics of the midpoints?"

"Well, you can only come to that if you realize that everything is designed according to aims. And aims need certain structures in order to be achieved. Everything that could not contribute is ignored.

An example: A question arises on a complex topic. You find an answer. As a result, you usually no longer include all the factors that could be considered for this question, but only those factors that support the answer you have decided on."

"Does that mean that the midpoint changes due to the determination?"

"Yes, first you were in the midpoint, which takes into account all the essential facts, then only those who supported your own opinion were seen."

"If you don't get the answer right, it would be a threat to the right answer," GP concluded.

"Exactly, all other essential factors are suddenly no longer taken into account."

"These are really interesting examples of how midpoint mechanics work," GP concluded thoughtfully.

Summarized:

How the brain works

> **The brain (which also contains the ego with its goals) interprets all information and makes all decisions based on the goals it contains – which include cognitive and intuitive parts.**

- **The brain directs and moves people.**

- **It is not that the brain is there on the one hand and the SELF is on the other, but this is integrated in the brain and plays its role from here.**

- **And to prevent a widespread misunderstanding: Consciousness is not the SELF!**

The brain is an interpreter: it interprets the world and events in a way that suits its aims. It has the task of interpreting perceptions and sensations (i.e. information) according to the aims it contains and generating appropriate attitudes and instructions for action.

(It does not simply depict the world, but shapes it - according to its aims.) This is done by the midpoints (neural networks).

This includes anticipating alternatives, and et al to ask the consciousness of what the particular problem solution might have consequences (so that it experiences it and gives information to the brain) - unless it already "knows" the consequences through similarities that it has stored.

Again: The brain does not simply depict the world, but shapes it - according to its aims. This is done by the neural networks (midpoints).

All human decisions are made by the brain in the head, the autonomic nervous system (plus the somatic nervous system), and the abdominal brain (enteric nervous system).

Between these there is a constant exchange of information by means of neural networks.

Anyone who has ever been in a research facility in which the constant firing of neurons is made audible, gets an impression of the countless processes that take place in the brain.

The general knitting pattern of the brain is the similarity; When an impulse, a question, a request, etc. comes up, it first looks for something that equals it.

The brain is subject to physical and chemical laws. It runs, as I said, for similarities, themes and aims with their midpoints that control it, and consists of various areas. For example, Amygdala, hippocampus, hypothalamus, cerebellum.

Certainly e.g., mainly activated by the eyes the visual center (occipital lobe) in the brain, by hearing the hearing center (the auditory cortex) etc., but also always neural networks (midpoints) at the same time.

The first is physical, the second psychic.

It is important to know that these areas never work separately for themselves, but always with others via neural networks.

These in turn have connections to many other networks, so that ultimately the entire brain in the head, the autonomic nervous system (plus the somatic nervous system) and the abdominal brain (enteric nervous system) are interconnected.

All networks were created by aims. The neurons located here are not only bound to them, but can also be used for others via synapses.

Networks are particularly activated by essential information of attention. The feelings that are always stimulated in parallel in the respective networks are of particular value. They are particularly suitable for controlling people. This functional process takes place through the respective similarities in the brain, which only include new information to a limited extent.

Like everything else, the brain runs on substances that are controlled by laws.

As already mentioned, the goals of the ego are also located in the brain. The ego consists of a relatively small number of goals, which - in terms of their values - represent an essential part of the brain. It can strengthen or weaken goals with its will and by means of information from perception, i.e. it can influence other goals in the brain via the midpoint mechanics of the will aim.

However: If you want something, a target can be activated or generated - but whether this works is decided by the psyche; and the then respectively activated midpoint in the brain.

One does not experience oneself as someone controlled by the brain; because one does not perceive its processes, except for the decisions; because of the diversity cannot perceive. Therefore, one has the impression that one decides oneself, with his free will, his consciousness.

Not least because of this, the general view is that man controls himself with his consciousness and that the brain is only an aid

So, we do not experience our brain, but what our senses convey to us via the brain.

People see, feel the result of their thinking, their actions and think that they did this (for example with their free will or with their consciousness).

They are wrong! That's what her brain did.

Because if you look more closely, you learn that you are not something separate from your brain that looks at the brain from the outside, but that you are integrated into it.

When one is observing oneself, the aim of observing that has formed as the midpoint in the brain is actually observing the brain.

I would like to point out again that consciousness in particular does not control people. This becomes clear when you take a closer look at consciousness, which is merely a supplier of information to the brain (so that it can make better decisions).

It can only come to someone from his brain. Even if something comes to mind from the environment, it is always up to the brain to decide what value it may have to be taken into account.

Ultimately, someone can only come up with something from their brain. Even if something comes to mind from the environment, it's always up to the brain to decide what value it might have in order to be considered.

Someone asked if one was a slave to his brain.

My Answer: The brain is not something alien, separate from the SELF - as the question sounded.

Without the brain, you are nothing. **With the brain**, one is everything that one feels, thinks, experiences, etc. daily. Here, too, are all the aims that the SELF wants to achieve.

And this will of the SELF can more or less bring the brain into corresponding structures with its midpoints via their mechanics, with appropriate practice and a favorable psyche.

One could only speak of slavery here if one has a weak will, or a strong (wilful) aim suppresses other (healthy) aims.

Everything that one perceives, recognizes, absorbs, thinks about, what comes to mind, etc., can form aims that reinforce others or generate new ones. Each new target creates or amplifies synapses, neural networks that work to achieve that aim. Once an aim has formed, it can play a role in the psyche.

The brain is constantly learning - by strengthening or rebuilding the synapses.

That's why it's so important to stay flexible in the brain (this is of course also an aim).

When a target is activated, such as when you want to grab a glass, then a trained cluster that consists of neural networks acts. This includes various areas in the brain to accomplish this task: estimating the distance to the glass, the size, weight, muscle and strength needed to lift it, etc. This is a brain work that we take for granted

As a rule, automatic, learned behaviours are used.

ings is their brains, which are capable of forming exorbitant neural networks with which they can recognize laws and create new processes.

And - with which an infinite number of fantasy structures can be imagined.

Yin and Yang

Behind this symbol is the striving for harmony in human beings: that feeling and reason (cognition) should be in an ideal relationship to each other.

This succeeds when both forces are of equal value; although they can act in opposite directions, they are not given an absolute striving for dominance.

So that they moderate and complement each other.

In order to achieve this, one should take a closer look with the mind at suspicious feelings that may be overwhelming but may not be so healthy:

• Which topic do you want to serve?

• Why are they pushing with such intensity?

If you do this several times in similar situations and offer alternatives, then you could modify the feelings with this tutorial.

Everyone has two sides: feeling and reason. Both are in the complex neural networks that ensure execution.

The art is to connect these two worlds with each other.

Feelings have ruled life since time immemorial. Initially, unicellular organisms formed. Much later multicellular organisms developed.

Two drivers prevailed here:

• The search for food sources

• And the preservation of life

The feeling developed about 3.5 billion years ago from the first moment in which life arose and wanted to be permanent.

All living beings arose with specific feelings (formed for survival). Insofar as they produced offspring, the feelings were also inherited.

The mind formed much later, particularly through competition with other living beings for survival resources.

Understanding means understanding a structure and its changes and drawing conclusions for yourself.

This is - in relation to feeling - a much more complicated and extensive area that took many millions of years to develop.

Feeling has settled into all areas as an element of life support and therefore plays a huge role. Especially since it can push people to do something.

However, it can neither think nor reflect; it is not intelligent. It only acts according to similarities in the past:

Feelings are therefore memories in order to react in identical situations in a consistent manner. What used to be positive or negative in the same situations is transferred to today and met with the appropriate behaviour. As a result, feelings can exert a strong pressure that resists cognitive attempts at change. But this can also lead to wrong behaviour; Because it makes you react inadequately to the current situation.

Feeling and reason are often opposed to each other as opposites.

As a rule, neither the one nor the other side is unreservedly 'right'. It follows that a union of these opposites should be striven for.

So, similar to how it is expressed in the Yin and Yang symbol.

Without one side, the other would be pretty much blind (also due to the midpoint-mechanic).

They should therefore be in a healthy balance as far as possible.

Epilogue

> **In closing, I would like to remind you in particular of these three natural foundations by which we are shaped (willingly or not):**

1. Deep drives in every human being

▶ **Life-complex**: To live as long as you can, regardless of the circumstances.

▶ **Producer-complex**: The mainspring to produce offspring, regardless of the environmental conditions.

▶ **Complex to follow someone**: the devotion to someone who is assigned special abilities and who is trusted to the point of blindness.

2. God

From the last (**Complex to follow someone**:), there is, with high probability, the actual cause from which the term "<u>God</u>" was formed.

As a rule, it is difficult to escape the feelings that have formed and embedded in the psyche from the beginning of the multicellular life to the present.

It would be helpful to use human cognitive abilities; But even with this, these feelings are often difficult to influence.

3. Naturally predetermined

The fact that everything had to happen the way it did is proven from two sides:

▶Identic parts under identical circumstances **always** result in identical structures.

▶Mathematicians can make very precise predictions about quantum systems using statistical probability calculations. This would not be feasible if lawlessness prevailed here.

And something else important:

It is often forgotten that people are only living beings that developed from inorganic substances and, like these, are shaped by laws. The main difference between inorganic and organic substances is **the goal of survival.**

The main difference between humans and other living beings is their brain, which is capable of forming exorbitant neural networks, with which they can recognize laws and create new processes.

And - with which an infinite number of imaginative structures can be fooled into him.

Such as the alleged role of consciousness:

In fact, up until the 23rd century, it was believed that consciousness is the real (objective) perception of the world believed to be from the human point of view, which the brain then absorbs:

Namely, that the environment sends stimuli that people's senses pick up and direct them to the inside of the brain, which uses them to recognize the world.

With this picture he would then have made his free decisions.

This kind of perception has never been scientifically proven.

In the end:

> Let me add a few basic words about the relationship between my (potential) readers and myself:
>
> People are guided by aims. These can or are influenced by the mid-point-mechanics. In such a way that what speaks against them is less or not at all noticed.
>
> As a rule, you do not notice these processes because they are part of the routine that the brain carries out on a daily basis.

This influence applies to a relative-ly large part of my representations regarding the perception of the readers.

For most, this is a description that doesn't fit their image of humanity.

That is unfortunate.

But I'm not interested in serving such expectations, but in writing what I've learned through my research.

Other books by me:

- Blindheit der Klugen
- Mittelpunkt der Psyche
- Midpoint of the psyche
- Die Entzauberung des Bewusst-
  seins (geänderte Auflage)
- The disenchantment of consci-
  ousness
- Was Gläubige wissen sollten
- What Believers Should Know
- Die Nicht-Entstehung des Uni-
  versums
- The non-creation of the uni-
  verse
- Wutgefühle: (Wie Gefühle ent-
  standen und den Menschen be-
  wegen)
- Feelings of anger: (How feel-
  ings arose and move people)
- Die Welt ohne Metaphysik: (Ei-
  ne klare Sicht auf den Men-
  schen und die Welt)
- The world without metaphysics:
  (A clear view of human and the
  world)
- 3 Gründe: Psychologische
  Grundlagen des Menschen ●●●
  Physikalische Grundlagen der
  Welt ●●● Betrachtungen des
  Glaubens
- 3 Basics of human beings